if you're clueless about mutual funds and want to know more

by SETH GODIN

Dearborn
Financial Publishing, Inc.®

If You're Clueless about Mutual Funds and Want to Know More

Executive Editor: Cynthia A. Zigmund
Managing Editor: Jack Kiburz
Interior and Cover Design: Karen Engelmann

Published by Dearborn Financial Publishing, Inc.®

Printed in the United States of America

97 98 99 10 9 8 7 6 5 4 3 2

Library of Congress Cataloging-in-Publication Data
Godin, Seth.
If you're clueless about mutual funds and want to know more / by Seth Godin.
p. cm.
Includes index.
ISBN 0-7931-2554-5 (paper)
1. Mutual funds--United States. I. Title.
HG4930.G63 1997
332.63'27--dc21 97-5610
CIP

Dearborn books are available at special quantity discounts to use as premiums and sales promotions, or for use in corporate training programs. For more information, please call the Special Sales Manager at 800-621-9621, ext. 4384, or write to Dearborn Financial Publishing, Inc., 155 North Wacker Drive, Chicago, IL 60606-1719.

Acknowledgments

Thanks to Jack Kiburz and Cindy Zigmund at Dearborn whose editorial guidance made this book possible. Karen Watts was the driving force behind the Clueless concept, and John Mello did an expert job of pulling it all together.

Thanks to Robin Dellabough, Lisa DiMona, Nana Sledzieski, Leslie Sharpe, Susan Kushnick, Lisa Lindsay, Julie Maner, and Sarah Silbert at SGP for their never-ending insight and hard work. And kudos to Sidney Short for his layout work, Theresa Casaboon for her copyediting talent, and Claire McKean for her expert proofreading.

Contents

GETTING *a clue* about *mutual* FUNDS

CHAPTER ONE

Y**ou may be clueless about* ***mutual funds, *but you're no dummy. When you think about it, you know you're actually sort of smart. So use those smarts to untangle the mysteries of the fund market and invest* ***wisely.***

You realize that it's time to think about your future, and you're doing something about it. You bought this book.

There was a time when mapping your future was a lot easier. You worked until 60 or 65 and then you spent 10 to 15 years on the shelf, basking in your golden retirement years. You knew that Social Security wouldn't make you rich, but you could expect that the check would be there every month like the phases of the moon. Your savings account performed cozily—even if it didn't rack up the earnings of today's red-hot technology stock. And although you might still have fretted about what was to be, you knew that if inertia got the best of you, chances were you'd still end up all right.

But now we live in the age of uncertainty. The good news is we're going to live longer. And a growing number of us will spend more time retired than we spent working. The bad news is that Social Security isn't the guarantee it used to be. And the earnings from that savings account can, at best, be characterized as paltry.

So you've got to take control. This book is a good first step toward that end because in The Information Age—the age we live in now—those who know will be living much more comfortably than those who know not. And those who can manage their money so it does what they want, when they want it done, will be living the most comfortably of all. Investing in mutual funds intelligently is a good way to make sure your money meets those expectations.

There were simpler times for investing in mutual funds, too. As recently as 15 years ago, there were only a few funds from which to choose. Now there are thousands. In fact, there are more mutual funds than there are companies on the New York Stock Exchange. These funds come in many flavors, based on investment objectives. And fund managers can control assets ranging in size from a meager $1 million to billions of dollars. You can buy funds from brokers, discount brokers, and financial planners. Some of the funds sell their products retail, or "over-the-counter." Even banks will sell them to you. All these factors add to the complexity of choosing funds for your portfolio and can make weeding out funds that are inappropriate seem like a chore. But all this will be easier for you after you read this book.

What Will You Learn Here?

In chapter two, you'll learn about stocks and bonds, which are the raw material for any mutual fund, and about market measures—like the Dow and S & P 500—against which fund performance is compared.

Then you'll learn why a mutual fund is good for you, how to determine your goals, and how to ascertain the risk level you feel comfortable with (chapter three).

By chapters four and five, you'll understand some of the basics. So we'll concentrate on explaining how funds are classified: the difference between open-end and closed-end funds, and how their values are set. You'll learn about types of funds: money market, income, growth and income, balanced, growth, index, sector, international, and tax-free funds.

You'll bone up on loads, too, the fees that mutual fund managers "load" onto your account for handling your money. In chapter six, you'll learn all about no-load funds, front-end loads, and back-end loads—and find out how to evaluate them when you're making investment decisions.

Mutual funds have advantages and disadvantages. To their credit, they're diversified. So by choosing them you aren't putting all your eggs into one basket. And your accounts are usually managed by top professionals. But there are risks and costs involved, as well. Weighing those negative factors against the positive aspects of investing is something we'll discuss in chapters seven and eight.

You'll also want to work with a company that values service, so in chapters nine and ten, we'll take a look at the different kinds of investment companies, accumulation plans, check-writing privileges, ways to move your money within a family of funds, and what kinds of fees you can expect to pay for your fund manager's efforts. And since research is important when you're choosing a fund, chapter eleven explains how to decipher a prospectus, the cornerstone of investment information.

Then there's the practical side of the whole process: how to open an account, register it, and make subsequent purchases, which you'll learn in chapters twelve and thirteen.

If you are like many investors, you'll soon stop feeling clueless about investing and begin to feel excited about the possibilities. In chapters fourteen, fifteen, and sixteen, we'll talk about devising investment strategies: Should you buy and hold your fund? Should you use dollar-cost averaging? How can you track your fund's performance in the newspapers and on the Internet? You'll also learn how to create a model portfolio and how to avoid the common mistakes investment tyros make.

Chapter seventeen explains basic tax issues, and how to gain tax relief through tax-free mutual funds. Finally, chapter eighteen will give you the push you need to get started.

There are over 8,000 mutual funds out there with a total value of $3 trillion. Understanding how to participate can help you harness that powerful force and get you closer to your financial goals. This is a great time to start investing in mutual funds—and this book will show you how to get a clue.

YOU'VE *heard* about stocks *and* BONDS

CHAPTER TWO

***W**hen you buy into a mutual fund, you're really buying a* **collection** *of stocks or bonds. Thousands of investors create a pool of money to tap into a huge well of securities. How they perform determines how much money you'll* **make.**

So it makes sense to know what a stock or bond really is, how the market sets their values, and where stocks are bought and sold.

An individual investor acting alone would be hard pressed to have the same success as a mutual fund company. A mutual fund marshals the financial resources of thousands of small investors and creates a pool of money to buy stocks and bonds. With this critical mass of money, a mutual fund can diversify its holdings and give an individual investor a measure of security that might otherwise be impossible to obtain.

The fund is run by an investment company, which hires a professional manager to oversee the conduct of the fund. The manager decides what stocks and bonds to buy based on the fund's objectives. The fund's objectives describe what it's trying to accomplish with its investments. A manager who is interested in growth, for example, would want the price of the stocks in the fund to increase rapidly. A manager who is interested in income would want holdings to produce high earnings or dividends for a fund's shareholders. The fundamental way a mutual fund makes money for you is based on how its holdings—its stocks and bonds—perform.

What's a Stock?

If you need money to buy a car or slap new gutters on your house, you might go to a bank for a loan. When a corporation needs money to improve business, it sells stock. A stock is, most simply, a piece of paper that proves you purchased a share, or a portion, of that company.

Corporations usually have thousands of shareholders, each of whom owns a fraction of the company. Each shareholder benefits from the company's successes, and bears the cost of its failures. Either scenario is reflected in the changing value of a stock as its price rises or falls. In fact, another reason companies issue stock is to share their financial risk in an unpredictable world. If you're very uncomfortable with this uncertainty, you can put all your money in a bank. But don't expect any big yields from a savings account. By accepting the risks of investing in stocks, shareholders also reap higher financial rewards.

NEVER FEEL BLUE WITH BLUE CHIPS

Blue-chip stocks get their name from the highest denomination of betting chip. The term was used as early as 1904 to identify high-priced, dividend-producing stocks of reputable corporations. In the United States, these companies are the **elite** of American industry, companies whose strength is unimpeachable.

It takes years for a stock to make it to the blue-chip pantheon. It needs to be seasoned, or proven stable over time. As the stock approaches blue-chip status, it may obtain other hues. If it's close to becoming a blue chip, it may be referred to as a **pale** blue chip. A little farther from exalted status, it might be called a white chip. Blue chips are sometimes referred to as bellwethers, stocks that lead the way up in rallies or down in declines. Just remember, the name comes from poker, which, the last time we checked, still involved gambling.

Just as corporations spread the risk among many shareholders, you can reduce your risk by investing in many different stocks. Buying into mutual funds lets you put your eggs in several baskets. Even if several stocks in the fund do poorly, the others may perform very well and offset any losses.

Companies can issue two kinds of stock: common and preferred. When you buy either kind of stock in a corporation, you become a partial owner of that corporation. But common stockholders are more directly connected to the fortunes of the company than preferred stockholders. That means that common stockholders have the potential to benefit from a company's growth when stock prices are high, but they have to take a backseat to preferred stockholders when any profits are distributed as dividends. (We'll talk about dividends later.)

Common stockholders have governing powers over the corporation. They have a say in the major policy decisions of the company—decisions about issuing more stock, selling the corporation to another company, or changing the board of directors, for example.

They also have the power to vote. In the political arena, if you're caught buying votes, you can end up in jail. In the corporate arena, everyone buys votes. That's one of the privileges of owning stock in a company. And although in a democracy it's considered bad form to digress from the one-person/one-vote principle, in the boardroom, it's considered good form. The number of votes stockholders have is usually pegged to how many shares of stock they own.

Stockholders can vote in person at the company's annual meeting. Most shareholders, though, vote by proxy, which is an absentee ballot that is mailed to shareholders before the meeting. There's even the equivalent of pulling the big lever on the voting machine and voting all Democrat or all

DOW MOMENTS

July 3, 1884—Dow Jones publishes its first average of U.S. stocks.

Jan. 12, 1906—Dow closes above 100 (100.25).

Oct. 28, 1929—The Dow drops 38.33 points (to 260.64) to start the Great Depression.

Republican because stockholders can check a box and rubber-stamp all the recommendations of the existing directors.

Although common stock is always found in the capital structure of a corporation, the same isn't true for preferred shares. The founding members usually determine whether or not a company will issue preferred shares when they write the company's charter. Just as a business may offer different consumer products to capture different market segments, a company may try to attract different kinds of investors by issuing different kinds of stocks. Preferred shares attract a different kind of investor than common shares do because they offer different benefits. Even though preferred shareholders don't usually have much to say about how a company is governed, they have first dibs on dividends if they're distributed by management—although the dividends are a fixed amount regardless of the company's performance. And if the company goes keel over smokestacks and its assets must be liquidated, preferred shareholders recover the money they've invested in the business before the holders of common shares do.

Corporations issue preferred shares after they issue common stock. They can also issue classes of common stock. These stocks are labeled A, B, and so forth. These have different prices, different dividend payments, and different conditions of ownership.

In general, a company issues different classes of stock to concentrate control of the firm in the

SEEING DOUBLE: STOCK SPLITS

Sometimes investors are too hot over the prospects of a company. They drive the price of a stock so high that **new blood** gets cool toward the issue. To make sure that doesn't happen, a company will split its stock.

So if you have 50 shares of XYZ Corp. selling at $100 a share and the company does a two-for-one split, you'll then own 100 shares worth $50 each.

Or if the stock split three-for-two, you'd have 75 shares of XYZ worth $66.66 a share.

If the stock split three-for-one, you'd have 150 shares worth $33.33 a share.

This may not seem much more than trading two nickels for a dime, but if the stock is as hot as it has been in the past, you may soon find it **selling at $100** again with you holding more shares.

Tier Structure

There's lots of ways to slice up stocks. One of them is by tiers. The four tiers of stocks are:

• **Blue Chips.** The killer elite of stocks; investing in blue chips is so safe it's almost like putting your money in a bank—only you'll earn more. But, as with any stock, you'll be taking on slightly more risk than you would if you had that money in the bank. Because sometimes, even the blue chips can fall. All the companies that make up the Dow Jones Industrial Average are considered blue-chip stocks.

• **Secondary Issues.** Solid, well-established companies that fall short of the blue-chip label in investors' minds. Microsoft and Apple Computing might be considered secondary issues—although Bill Gates and Gilbert Amelio might debate the point.

• **Growth Stocks.** Emerging companies with growth potential but no assurances of success. A classic example of a growth stock would be Netscape. Most biotech issues fall into this category, too.

• **Penny Stocks.** Long shots; companies with no value other than their speculative potential. You probably haven't heard of any of these companies and neither has any mutual fund manager you're likely to work with. These stocks are for speculators, and people who spend a lot of time at the track.

For the most part, you can tell which tier a company fits in by its credit ratings. The chief credit rating outfits are Standard & Poor's and Moody's.

FALLING, FOR NOW

Each day, the **average price** of all the stocks on the market is reported to the public. Although stock averages always change, it can give you quite a scare when the average price of a stock falls dramatically, as it sometimes does. Here are some of the **largest drops** in the Nasdaq Composite Index:

Date	Drop
Oct. 19, 1987	46.12
July 15, 1996	43.11
July 19, 1995	35.70
July 11, 1996	34.83
Jan. 9, 1996	33.56
Oct. 20, 1987	32.42
July 23, 1996	32.32
Oct. 26, 1987	29.55
Dec. 18, 1995	27.92
Oct. 9, 1995	27.30

hands of a preferred set of stockholders, most often the founders of the business. In 1986, for example, Chris-Craft Industries issued a new class of common stock to its existing stockholders. For each share of existing common stock, a shareholder received two shares of Class B stock. Each B share had supervoting rights that allowed holders of the stock to have ten votes per share. The net effect was that the original shareholders would have control of the company because future investors were limited to buying only regular common shares, which gave them one vote per share.

For the most part, stock classes need not concern a mutual fund investor since funds usually invest only in common stock.

How Do You Make Money Investing in Stocks?

Usually, the more profit a company makes, the more money you, as the stockholder, make. You can receive that money by selling the stock for more than you paid for it, or by receiving dividend payments while you own the stock.

What's a Dividend Payment?

Many companies divvy up their profits in the form of quarterly dividend payments—which are frequently mailed to the shareholder as a check (although they may be reinvested in additional shares of stock). When the profit is shared among thousands of stockholders, the dividend on a single share may seem minuscule. But the dollar value naturally goes up if you own many shares, and dividends that are reinvested ultimately increase the base value of the stock portfolio.

Dividends vary from stock to stock. Those that consistently pay high dividends are called income stocks. Their stock prices are relatively stable and you continue to own them because you expect to receive a dividend check as regularly as you expect your bank to pay interest on your savings account.

But, unlike a bank, a company doesn't have to pay dividends. It can decide to use the money in other ways, such as to grow the company. A company that pays little or no dividends is called a growth company. Hopefully, as the company grows, so will the price of its stock. When it reaches a level that's attractive to you, you can sell it and make a tidy profit.

How Are Stock Prices Determined?

Although you can profit from selling a stock, changing stock prices make for a less predictable income than dividend checks. Stocks don't have a fixed worth. They're only as valuable as people believe they are from moment to moment. When many people believe the stock market is going to do well, they invest enthusiastically and aggressively—the overall trend is known as a bull market. A trend of shyer, more cautious investing is known as a bear market.

When you speculate in a stock, you're making a bet that a lot of people are going to want to buy that stock after you do. If they do, the price of the stock will go up and you'll be able to cash in. It's a gamble, but the odds are better than lotto.

HOW WALL STREET GOT ITS NAME

There are certain street names in this world that have become synonymous with the industries that reside on them. When you hear **"Madison Avenue,"** you think advertising. When you say "Wall Street," people know you mean business. Historically, it was named for the stockade built there by settlers to protect the city from invasion from the north by pirates and Indians.

You can also gamble that a lot of people aren't going to want a stock. That's called shorting a stock. When you short a stock, you borrow shares from your broker and sell them at the current market price. Then you wait and hope the price of the stock drops. While you're waiting for the price to drop, your broker is collecting interest on the value of the transaction. You bank on the hope that the drop in stock price will cover the interest payments and net you a profit. Here's how a simple short sale might work.

You borrow 100 shares of a company called Cyberkon for $10 a share. You sell the stock and pocket $1,000. Two weeks later, the price of Cyberkon stock drops to $8 a share. You purchase your borrowed shares for $800 (100 x 8) and make $200 less the interest payments you had to pay the broker.

Calculating the odds of a stock transaction is different from placing bets at the track. In the sport of kings, the more people who bet on a horse, the lower the odds are on that horse (because the winnings must be shared by a larger number of people). But if many people "bet" on a stock, it is viewed as increasing in value. So the price goes up and you can make more money.

Underlying the stock, of course, is a company. And how that company makes money has less to do with the roll of the dice or the luck of the draw. Traders know that. So do stock analysts, people whose livelihood depends on their ability to judge a company's prospects. They project earnings. They evaluate the products a company makes and analyze if anyone wants to buy them. They look at competitors. And they look at who's running a company. You can do these things, too. But if you don't have an inclination to do so, you can have a mutual fund manager and his team of financial professionals do it for you by buying into the fund.

DOW MOMENTS

Mar. 12, 1956—Dow closes above 500 (500.24).

Nov. 14, 1972—Dow closes above 1,000 (1,003.16).

Aug. 17, 1982—Dow climbs 38.81 (to 831.24), its biggest ever one-day gain, signaling the start of the '80s bull market.

Where Are Stocks Sold?

Stock exchanges are organizations that bring professional stock traders together so they can buy and sell stocks in a regulated way. Companies that want to sell stock are admitted to the organization after meeting certain criteria based on location, company size, and financial earnings.

There are scores of exchanges throughout the world, but the two that you're probably most familiar with are the New York and American. Most stocks in the United States, however, aren't traded on an exchange at all but in the over-the-counter (OTC) market.

The OTC is basically a nerd's dream. Traders never meet face-to-face. All their work is done from a computer screen or a telephone.

OTC traders are regulated by an organization called the National Association of Securities Dealers, or NASD. And the listings of their stocks appear in the newspaper under the heading Nasdaq—the National Association of Securities Dealers Automated Quotations.

The Nasdaq Stock Market lists over 5,120 domestic and foreign companies, more companies than any other stock market in the world. Nasdaq's share volume reached 101.2 billion shares in 1995 and its dollar volume reached $2.39 trillion. In 1995, the Nasdaq share volume surpassed that of all other U.S. stock markets.

The over-the-counter market is sort of a catchall for all trading not done on a registered exchange like the New York and American stock exchanges.

NOT READY FOR TAILS TIME

There was a time when the New York Stock Exchange maintained strict decorum. Its members wore top hats and swallowtail coats and were encouraged to present themselves in a respectable manner. Those who didn't were fined. Reprehensible behavior and the punishment for members who persisted in it were as follows:

- Smoking a **cigar:** $5
- Standing on a **chair:** $10
- **Throwing** a paper dart: $10
- Knocking off a member's **hat:** $.50

A registered exchange is an auction marketplace—all trading takes place at a single location. The over-the-counter market is a negotiated marketplace—trading can take place anywhere there's a buyer and seller. For that reason, trading numbers from day-to-day OTC activity are best guesses on how a security fared.

The Nasdaq is a convenient way to conduct over-the-counter business because it has what's called market makers for stocks. These brokers have pledged to provide continuing bids and offerings on a particular issue. This saves your broker time searching high and low for someone to buy stock from or sell stock to. So if you want to buy 100 shares of Microsoft, for example, your broker can go to a market maker for Microsoft on the Nasdaq and buy the shares from her. Otherwise, your broker would have to search for someone who wanted to sell 100 shares of Microsoft. It might so happen your broker has 100 shares of Microsoft he wants to sell or knows someone who wants to part with some Microsoft stock. In that case, the broker could make the trade without dealing with a market maker.

MULTIPLE DOWS

There are actually **four** Dow Jones averages. **The Dow Jones Industrials** is the one most often quoted in newscasts and what people are referring to when they say, "The Dow was up," or "The Dow was down today." **The Dow Jones Transportation Average** contains stocks from airlines, trucking companies, and railroads. **The Dow Jones Utility Average** tracks gas and electric companies. **The Dow Jones Composite Average** takes all the stocks in the other averages and creates a composite picture of them.

Although over-the-counter business is conducted through the Nasdaq, not all over-the-counter business is conducted there. For example, there are also private transactions by public investors that aren't reported to the Nasdaq.

The New York Stock Exchange, also known as The Big Board, isn't the oldest—Philadelphia's exchange was organized in 1790—but it is probably the world's most famous exchange. It began modestly enough in 1792 under a Buttonwood tree in front of 68 Wall Street where 24 brokers agreed to favor each other in trading and accept nothing less than a quarter of a percent commission on trade. Today about 51 million individual investors and several thousand institutional investors are buyers and sellers of securities issued by more than 2,500 listed companies on the New York Stock Exchange.

The New York exchange operated without competition until the New York Curb Exchange was founded in 1842. True to its name, it traded in the streets until it moved indoors in 1921, and it eventually became known as the American Stock Exchange.

Trading, literally on the street, led to a rough-and-tumble existence and an unsavory reputation. In polite company, one just didn't admit to brushing shoulders with the curbside crowd. A famous anecdote about the species goes something like this:

A trader attending a society shindig found himself sitting beside a woman sophisticate who asked him, "What do you think of Balzac, sir?" "Well, ma'am," the trader replied, "I never trade in them Curb stocks."

From its beginnings in the gutter, the American Stock Exchange has grown to represent the stocks of more than 700 companies and has become the world's second largest auction marketplace. It was also the first stock exchange to go on the World Wide Web. Although the AMEX (www.amex.com) may have been the first exchange to have a Web presence, the Nasdaq (www.nasdaq.com) Web site has much more "live" information such as stock quotes and mutual fund net asset values.

What's a Bond?

Think of a bond as a "pinstripe IOU." Although selling shares of stock is a good way for companies to raise money, it isn't the only way. Companies can sell bonds, too. Bonds are simply IOUs that a company issues when you lend it money, and bonds can make up some or all of a mutual fund you decide to purchase.

DOW MOMENTS

Jan. 8, 1987—Dow breaks the 2,000 mark for the first time (2,002.25).

July 17, 1987—Dow closes above 2,500 (2,510.04).

Oct. 16, 1987—The Dow falls 108.35 (to 2,246.73), the first time the Dow has ever fallen 100 points.

Bonds are debt. And the conditions of the debt to the bondholder are set by the company. For the investor, this is very different from buying stocks. Stock gives you equity in the company. It makes you a beneficiary of the company's success. Bonds make you a creditor. Every bond has three essential pieces of information:

Par Value

Par value is the amount the bondholder will be paid when the bond reaches maturity. This is the equivalent of the principal on a loan. So if the par value of the bond is $1,000, that is the amount you will be paid when the bond matures. It's also the amount you paid for the bond.

Interest Rate

The interest rate is the percentage of the par value that the bond pays you periodically until its maturity date. This is the equivalent of the interest rate you would pay on a loan or mortgage. So if the interest rate on a $1,000 bond is 12 3/8 percent a year, you would receive $123.75 annually from the bond until it expired.

Another term for the interest rate on a bond is the coupon. The term originates with the coupons that used to be attached to all bonds when you received them. Each coupon represented an interest payment to you. When it was time to collect a payment, you would clip the coupon, send it in to the company, and they would send you your money. It's like the coupon book some lenders issue with their mortgages. Only instead of mailing in a coupon and a mortgage payment, you mail in the coupon and a payment is mailed to you.

SEEING PINK

Some low-priced stocks aren't listed in the newspapers because they're not on the Nasdaq system. They're **thinly traded.** That means their volumes may be in the hundreds rather than the thousands. And they may be selling for less than the worth of the paper a stock certificate is printed on, sometimes less than one cent a share. Usually only brokers receive the daily listings of these stocks that are printed on pink sheets of paper—hence, the name **"pink sheets."**

Maturity

This is the date when the issuer of the bond agrees to pay you its par value. Maturities can vary widely. The shorter the maturity date the less risk there is to you. That's because the chances of something happening in six months to prevent a company from paying back par value on a bond is far less than the chances of something happening to a company in 40 years. On the other hand, the shorter the maturity term, the lower the interest rate on the bond will be.

Unlike the vagaries of stocks, bonds pay a fixed rate of interest. You may ask, then why do bond prices change? The answer is, although the interest rate on the bond is fixed, interest rates in the market are not. Assume you buy a $1,000 bond from XYZ Corp. that pays 6.75 percent interest. If, by the time you are ready to sell your bond, the prevailing interest rates rise to 8 percent, few people will want to buy the bond you're holding if it only earns the lower rate. That kind of scenario would discourage people from lending their money. You'd have to sell it at a discount, or at less than par value.

But if interest rates decline to, say, 5.50 percent, then your bond, which pays 1.25 more than the going rate, will look attractive to an investor. You will be able to sell your bond at a premium, or more than its par value.

That's why there's a difference between a bond's yield, and its interest rate. Your $1,000 bond with a 6.75 percent interest rate earns you $67.50 a year. But if you had to sell the bond at a discount, say, for $800, the yield for the buyer of the bond is going to be greater than 6.75 percent. That's because the buyer will continue to collect $67.50 a year, which is 8.44 percent of an $800 investment.

The opposite is true if you sold the bond at a premium. In that case, the buyer's yield would be less than 6.75 percent. So if you sold your 6.75

NET ASSET VALUE

Imaginary Investments has a portfolio with 50 stocks. On a given day the total value of those stocks is $100 million. There are 10 million **outstanding** shares. The NAV (net asset value) for that day would be $10 per share ($100 million divided by 10 million). If you owned 20 shares of this portfolio, they would be worth $200 on that day.

percent bond at $1,200 because the prevailing interest rate was at 5.50 percent, the buyer's yield on the bond would be 5.625 percent.

Measuring Performance

Everyone with an interest in the stock market wants to know how it is going to perform. And as a mutual fund investor, you'll want to know because, as we mentioned earlier, mutual funds are collections of stocks. Some people believe they can predict trends in the market by keeping close tabs on certain major market indicators. Here are some of the indicators you should be familiar with:

The Dow Jones Industrial Average

This, the king of indicators, is calculated minute-by-minute and is published by Dow Jones & Co. The companies that make up the Dow are chosen for their intimate connection with the economic lifeblood of the nation. That connection has proven to be pretty good in determining the pulse of the market.

Over the past century "the Dow," as it is known, has become the most widely recognized stock market indicator in the United States, and probably in the world. The 30 stocks included in the Dow are listed on the New York Stock Exchange and can be characterized as very large, healthy, and stable companies that reflect the health of the U.S. economy. All but a handful of these have major business operations throughout the rest of the world, thus also providing some insight into the economic well-being of the global economy.

The Dow is also the longest established of all share indexes. It can trace its origins back to 1897—when it was calculated using just 12 stocks—and has been the role model for some of the world's other leading indexes, such as the Nikkei 225 in Tokyo.

Today's 30 constituents are chosen by Dow Jones and *The Wall Street Journal* to represent a balanced selection of top-notch stocks. In recent years, the composition has been gradually altered, to reflect the shift in the U.S. economy away from traditional manufacturing and toward computers and service industries.

The Difference Between Stocks and Mutual Funds

	Stocks	Mutual Funds
What You Buy	Shares of a single company.	Shares in a fund, which is a collection of stocks and bonds.
Voting Rights	Yes.	No.
What You Pay	Dictated by the market price of a share.	You can invest any amount provided it's above the minimum.
Who Decides?	You and your broker decide when to buy and sell.	The fund manager decides how to set up and trade the portfolio. You decide when to buy or sell your shares.
Any Goodies?	Dividends are paid directly to you or to your brokerage firm for you.	You decide how to reinvest dividends and interest payments. Dividends can be reinvested to purchase more shares or be paid directly to you as cash.
How Liquid Is It When You Sell?	You must wait five business days.	In some cases, you can have your money the next business day. Legally, proceeds must be available within seven days. You can move money among funds quickly.

HEDGING YOUR BETS

A mutual fund diversifies your investment, just as it would if you were to buy stocks in several different companies. Say your mutual fund buys 100 shares of the following companies: Hook Brewery at $13 a share; Motorola at $55; Microsoft at $155; Netscape at $57; and Sam Adams Brewery at $11. Your total outlay is $29,100 with an average per share price of $58.20.

Six months later, you check the stocks for each company and discover that Hook has dropped to $11 a share and Sam Adams is trading at $10. But Microsoft has climbed to $160, Motorola to $60, and Netscape to $65.

You experience some losses, but **your gains** more than cover them. Your portfolio is now worth $30,600, a gain worth a little over 5 percent. Not bad for six months and certainly better than putting all your eggs in one basket.

Five years ago, the editors of *The Wall Street Journal* added Walt Disney and J. P. Morgan to the average in order to reflect the shift in the U.S. economy to services in general and entertainment in particular. Both of these new additions also conduct major operations worldwide. The editors of *The Wall Street Journal* have always thought of the Dow "industrials" as meaning more than manufacturing, and the service sector of the economy has been reflected in the Dow average since 1928 with stocks such as Sears and Woolworth.

Though it has only 30 stocks, the Dow Industrial Average's tracking of market moves over the long run closely parallels indexes with hundreds and even thousands of stocks, such as Standard & Poor's 500 stock index and the Wilshire 5000.

Standard & Poor's 500

Introduced in 1957, the S & P 500 consists of a broad range of 500 stocks. Since some stocks influence the market more than others, those stocks are weighted when figuring out this indicator. Like the Dow, the S & P is also broken into smaller industrial segments. This indicator is often used as a measure of a fund's performance. People ask, "Did it do better than the S & P 500?" Many funds don't.

The Nasdaq Composite

Since the OTC market is crowded with startup companies and speculative stocks, fluctuations in this index are usually interpreted as a measure of investors' enthusiasm for small stocks and their willingness to take risks on the economy.

What Are "the Dow" Averages?

The famous Dow averages are calculated to help investors gauge the overall strength or weakness of the American economy. They are composed of three primary indexes: the Industrial Average, the Transportation Average, and the Utilities Average. Here are the companies used to compile the index you most often hear about, the Dow Jones Industrial Average.

Allied Signal
Aluminum Co. of America
American Express
AT&T
Bethlehem Steel
Boeing
Caterpillar
Chevron
Coca-Cola
Walt Disney
DuPont
Eastman Kodak
Exxon
General Electric
General Motors
Goodyear Tire and Rubber
IBM
International Paper
McDonald's
Merck
Minnesota Mining & Manufacturing
J. P. Morgan
Philip Morris
Procter and Gamble
Sears Roebuck
Texaco
Union Carbide
United Technologies
Westinghouse Electric
Woolworth

AMEX Composite Index

On January 2, 1997, the American Stock Exchange introduced a new AMEX Composite Index with a new ticker symbol, XAX. It replaced the former AMEX Market Value Index (XAM) which, since its inception, was calculated on a "total return basis" to include the reinvestment of dividends paid by AMEX companies. The new AMEX Composite Index will be more comparable with other major indexes, which reflect only the price appreciation of their respective components.

In addition, the AMEX introduced five subindexes that will track the performance of companies in key AMEX market sectors: information technologies (ticker symbol XIT), financial (ticker symbol XFI), healthcare (ticker symbol XHL), natural resources (ticker symbol XNA), and industrials (ticker symbol XID).

Now that we've got down some basics about stocks, bonds, and markets, let's explore what mutual funds are all about.

A primer on mutual FUNDS

CHAPTER THREE

Mutual funds are relatively new investment **options** *that have popularized financial planning and have made investing easy for millions of people who would not have bought stocks and bonds* **otherwise.**

Mutual funds were first started in the 1920s, but the reason you hear so much about them lately is that they make investing very accessible and less intimidating to the average person.

Consider that if you want to enter the stock market on your own, by buying individual stocks, you need about $100,000 to properly diversify your portfolio. Then you have to research your stocks and bonds. And once you buy your stocks, you have to continue to watch them to make sure they're performing the way you want them to. Even if you've got the money to create your portfolio, chances are you don't have the time to manage it. Investing in mutual funds simplifies all that. And this chapter will help you understand why.

Ante Up, You're in the Pool

When you invest in a mutual fund, you don't need a lot of money to start because you pool your resources with other investors. And your risk is spread out over several stocks.

Fund managers combine your money with money from other investors to buy a collection of securities that is managed by a professional investment company. The company usually has teams of in-house analysts and research staffs that constantly monitor economic and financial data. They answer to fund managers, who are ultimately responsible for the success or failure of funds.

As powerful as the fund managers and analysts can be, they don't have carte blanche. They still must follow the objectives of the fund—their promise to you, the investor—and aim to select securities that represent the best opportunities for achieving those objectives. In addition, the fund companies dangle financial incentive carrots in the faces of their portfolio managers to encourage them to outperform the market. Those incentives include a cut of the funds' management fees, substantial chunks of cash that become even more substantial as the assets of the funds grow.

Mutual funds have gained popularity because there's safety in numbers. Since large numbers of investors contribute to the fund, it's easy for even Mr. and Mrs. Sixpack to enter the market. Average investors can get in inexpensively and work on increasing their shares in the fund in small increments.

The securities purchased by the fund make up its portfolio. Funds invest in stocks, bonds, money market instruments such as certificates of deposit, and other kinds of assets. The fund receives income from interest payments and dividends or by reaping capital gains from the sale of stocks. These are distributed to the shareholders of the fund. Or they can request that earnings be reinvested into the fund so they can buy more shares.

What Makes the Money Grow?

Your mutual fund investment grows through the distribution of dividends and capital gains by the fund. Dividends and capital gains are paid out to shareholders in proportion to the number of fund shares they own. Whether you've got $100 or $100,000 in the fund, your return on the dollar will be the same.

Fund managers buy and sell the securities in a fund. When they sell a security for more than they bought it for, they make a profit, or capital gain, just as they do when they make a profit on a stock. These capital gains are distributed to everyone with shares in the fund.

Each share in a fund you buy represents your proportional share of all the stocks and bonds that make up the fund. Most funds have 50 to 100 securities in them. When you buy into the fund, you're buying a piece of all of them, or a share. A share's worth is the total value of all the securities in the fund divided by the outstanding shares. The worth of a single share of a fund is called the net asset value, commonly referred to as NAV.

The NAV changes from day to day as the value of the securities in a fund's portfolio change. So on any day, your shares in your fund may be worth more or less than what you originally paid for them.

A Historical Perspective

In 1908, an automobile was something only wealthy Americans could hope to own. But after Henry Ford's first Model T rolled off the assembly line that year, the United States became a nation of motorists. Sixteen years later, in March 1924, Massachusetts Investors Trust established the

PAYING THE PIPER

Fund loads can range from 2 percent to 8.5 percent. Front-end load funds charge you when you enter the fund. **Back-end load** funds charge you when you exit the fund.

A contingent deferred sales charge, which ranges from 1 percent to 6 percent, is levied when you cash out but usually decreases over time. The idea is to **discourage investors** from using the fund as a short-term investment.

Funds also charge management fees—usually a half of a percent or less, depending on the assets of the fund.

A 12b-1, or **sales distribution fee,** may also be charged. This fee ranges from a quarter of a percent to 1 percent and is used to pay for the promotion and distribution of fund shares.

Expect to pay roughly 1 to 2 percent for expenses and fees.

It's the Law

When you turn your money over to someone else to handle, it's reassuring to know that laws have been written to protect you.

The Securities Act of 1933 requires investment companies to register their funds with the Securities and Exchange Commission.

The Securities Exchange Act of 1934 protects investors against fraud. Institutions and people who sell mutual funds are regulated by both the Securities and Exchange Commission and the National Association of Securities Dealers. Ground rules have been established for the fair treatment of the public and prohibit such activity as manipulating security prices and using misleading and fraudulent devices to influence stock prices.

The Investment Company Act of 1940. This act prohibits self-dealing by those who work for the mutual fund company. Fund officers also must carry fidelity bond coverage if they have access to the investment companies' securities. The act places limits on bond fees and commissions that shareholders may pay.

nation's first mutual fund in Boston. By year's end the fund had attracted 200 investors and $392,000. But it took a little longer for the country to become a nation of mutual fund buyers.

By 1929, there were 19 mutual funds with assets of about $140 million. During the Depression years, growth was understandably slow. In 1940, the combined assets of the 68 funds in existence totaled less than $500 million.

From 1950 to 1980, the industry heated up. By the end of 1972, there were over 400 mutual funds with assets over $60 billion and more than 10 million shareholder accounts. In 1986, the number of mutual funds had grown to 1,900 and investors had poured $708 billion more into them.

In just three decades, the whole category of mutual funds has risen from an "also ran" in the race for America's investment money to national ascendancy. In 1965, fund assets of $48 billion were but 10 percent of savings in banks ($457 billion); at year-end 1993, bank savings totaled $2.3 trillion, just narrowly ahead of the then $2.0 trillion total for mutual funds. And today fund assets total more than $3.5 trillion.

For 30 years, mutual funds have been growing, and financial market returns soared to record levels. Even the government contributed to making conditions favorable for funds. It changed the law so that municipal bond funds could be set up to shelter income from taxes. And it created a new retirement animal called the Individual Retirement Account, which created a tax-beneficial method for the average person to supplement the money that could be expected from pensions. The goverment also created the 401(k) thrift plan, which enables companies to set up retirement accounts for their employees (usually as mutual funds). Companies have seized upon this option fervently—assets now comprise $800 billion of the mutual fund industry's $3.5 trillion total.

AN OLD IDEA

The oldest stock exchange in the world is the **London Stock Exchange,** which was officially established in 1773 although its origins date back to 100 years before that. Paris founded its exchange in 1802, New York in 1817, Tokyo in 1818, and Sydney in 1872.

These changes had a significant impact on the nature of the mutual fund industry. They helped shift its asset base from one that was virtually all equities, or stocks, to a more diversified base comprised of equity funds (39 percent of industry assets), bond funds (33 percent), and money market funds (28 percent). That diversification of the industry's asset base, in turn, helps draw more money into the funds as well as broadens its customer base from the very small investor to the very large institution.

It is important to note that, in their heyday in the early 1980s, 75 percent of mutual fund assets were in money market funds. Because money markets are relatively safe investment vehicles, this gave the industry its first taste of savings (as distinguished from investment) "blood." In 1983, as interest rates fell, banks received the authority to pay current money market rates on their savings accounts, so the growth rate of money market funds ebbed. But the near-contemporaneous beginning of the stock and bond bull markets of virtually unprecedented magnitude quickly took up the industry's slack. Today, investors can select mutual funds that invest much more aggressively, if they choose, making the mutual fund market a sensible and potentially profitable investment option.

Cautionary Notes

Choosing a mutual fund to suit your financial needs will take a little mental exercise, but with the thousands of funds out there, there's little doubt you'll be able to find a flavor that will satisfy your financial palate. Before you start your search, however, here are a few things you should keep in mind.

- Mutual funds are not get-rich-quick investments. If you're looking for a fast financial fix, you should start a company making something for the Internet and go public—that is, sell stock to the public through an initial public offering—as soon as possible. Or you could play the lottery.

- Mutual funds aren't entirely risk-free, but they are strictly regulated and controlled.

- Mutual funds aren't designed to be held for the short term. When you buy into one, expect to hold on to your investment for a while.

- Mutual fund shares don't usually make large moves up or down. If you want to play with your money, you don't want a mutual fund. A mutual fund is not a toy. It's especially not a yo-yo.

- A mutual fund is a convenient and sensible way for a tyro to enter the investment field. Most funds are relatively safe, well-managed, well-regulated, diversified investment vehicles. There are so many of them, and they're so varied and accessible that there's bound to be one available to meet your investment goals.

Why Invest in Mutual Funds?

- Mutual funds are managed by professionals. They do this for a living and how well a living they make from it depends on how fat they make your investment.

- A mutual fund lets you share the danger by diversifying your investment. Financial research shows that 60 percent of the time, a stock's price is going to move up and down with the overall stock market. This is known as market risk. Another 20 to 30 percent of the time, a stock's price is determined by traders' reactions to industry news or to news about the specific company. The remaining 10 percent or so has to do with dumb luck or fate. Investing in the stock market carries with it a certain degree of unpredictability. A mutual fund tempers your risk.

- A mutual fund lets you hedge your bets, so to speak. A fund with 50 to 100 stocks won't be hurt if one or two companies turn sour and the price of their stocks goes south.

- The rule of thumb is the more stocks you have in the portfolio, the lower the risk in the portfolio. Mutual funds give you an automatic portfolio.

- Although diversification helps reduce risk, it doesn't erase it. And since a large percentage of stocks move with the market, market risk always looms over your portfolio, especially if your portfolio only has stocks in it. There are other kinds of assets that aren't as susceptible to this kind of market risk: bonds, money funds, precious metals, and stock in foreign companies.

- Mutual funds have demonstrated good long-term performance. That's particularly true for funds that invest in stocks. Stocks go up, stocks go down, but overall they tend to go up. From 1926 to 1992, for example, the S & P 500 earned a compound rate of 10.3 percent. That compares very favorably with long-term corporate bonds (5.4 percent), long-term government bonds (4.9 percent), and U.S. Treasury bills (3.7 percent).

- What good is having money if you can't get your hands on it? Mutual funds allow you to redeem your shares by telephone and write checks on your accounts. It's also easy to move money within a family of funds. This can come in handy when investment conditions change. For example, in 1982 when double-digit interest rates began to decline, investors began moving their cash out of money market funds and into equity funds, as Wall Street started to resemble Pamplona, where the bulls run rampant.

- Buying in to a mutual fund is a relatively low-cost investment. You can invest as little as $200 in a fund and make subsequent investments of just $50 each.

- Mutual funds allow you to make automatic investments and systematic withdrawals. You can arrange to have your bank electronically transfer a fixed amount of money or a percentage of an account to your mutual fund each month or pay period. You can also arrange to have money systematically withdrawn from the mutual fund. This is frequently done by retired people to supplement their incomes. The percentage you can withdraw varies depending upon the fund.

- Mutual funds are regulated by the federal Securities and Exchange Commission. All funds are required by law to disclose the same information in the same form in a document called a prospectus.

- You don't have to worry about a mutual fund going bankrupt because the fund can never lose more money than it has in assets. The value of your investment can drop if the value of the securities in the fund's portfolio declines, but the fund never gets into a situation where its liabilities exceed it assets. That's what happens when a company goes bankrupt or a bank crashes. If too many people try to withdraw their money from a bank at the same time, the bank sinks because, on average, only 20 cents of every dollar deposited is on hand in cash. The rest of the money has been invested in loans. If a run were made on a mutual fund, all the investors would receive every penny their shares were worth when they redeemed them because the fund has a dollar's worth of securities for every dollar it owes its investors. If it is any further consolation, since the passage of the Investment Company Act of 1940 (the act regulating mutual funds), no fund has ever gone under.

Even if the sponsor of the fund starts taking on water, you're still in the clear. By law, your fund is a separate company outside the grasping claws of creditors.

- There are federal laws protecting you from fraud and deception, but there are no laws protecting you from making bonehead investments. If you invest in a high-risk fund and lose your shirt, you won't have recourse in a court of law.

You Pick 'Em

How do you pick a mutual fund? One of the first things you should consider is whether the fund has a load or not. When you choose a fund with a load, you lose money the minute you write your check to the fund sponsor.

Load funds are sold to investors by brokerage firms. When you buy a fund with a load you pay

DOW MOMENTS

Oct. 19, 1987—The Dow plunges 508 to 1,738.74 in what has become known as "Black Monday."

Jan. 2, 1990—Dow sets a new record at 2,810.15—the new all-time high.

Apr. 17, 1991—Dow closes over 3,000 (3,004.46).

the net asset value for each share you purchase plus a sales commission, which is the load. Load amounts vary. They may be as high as 8.5 percent or as low as 2.5 percent of your total purchase. Even when you buy a fund with a load directly from a fund's sponsor, the load is collected.

No-load funds sell their shares directly to the public at net asset value. Since there is no middleman involved, there are no sales charges. The advantage of a no-load fund is that from day one you have 100 percent of your investment working for you, not 100 minus 8.5 or 2.5 or whatever percentage the load may be. For example, when you invest $10,000 in a fund with a load of 8.5 percent, $9,150 is deposited into your account. When you invest $10,000 into a no-load fund, $10,000 is sent to your account. Since you start with less money in your account with the load fund, your overall earnings for the time you are in the fund are less than they would be if they were in a no-load fund.

Why buy a load fund? Brokers say you're paying for service. But studies have shown that there is no significant correlation between sales charges and performance.

Goals

The next step in choosing a fund is to identify your investment goals. Your overall goal is to make money, but it's wise to narrow things down a bit.

There are two kinds of goals: general goals and specific goals. Are you looking for your fund to generate income through dividends and earnings? Do you want your investment to grow? Are you looking for a shelter from Uncle Sam? Those are general goals. Do you need a down payment for a house or car? Do you want to create a college fund for a child? Are you saving for retirement? Those are specific goals.

Why do you need goals? Because what your goals are determine the type of fund to invest your money in. It doesn't make sense to put a pot of money into a fund loaded with growth stocks if your goal is to buy a house. The stock market can be volatile over the short run, and when the time comes to use the money for its purpose, the cash may not be there. However, if you're investing for a long-term goal—college tuition for a child or retirement—then investing in a fund subject to the vagaries of the market would be appropriate because over time, the ups and downs of the market even out.

Risky Business

The thought of putting savings into anything but a bank can be frightening to some of us. Putting them into stocks can be absolutely terrifying. Everyone knows about the great market crashes. It's scary to think about how long it took to regain the value lost in those crashes. So after you've figured out your financial goals, it's a good idea to take the pulse of your attitude toward risk.

Although mutual funds do a good job of minimizing risk, they don't eliminate it. So before you buy into a type of fund, you should be aware of how much risk you can take. Such an assessment can save you some money in headache medicine and gastrointestinal palliatives later on.

There are lots of tests floating around that will help you determine your risk tolerance. We've included one from Ameristock Mutual Fund.

Circle the numbers that correspond to your responses to the questions.

I plan on using my money:

After seven years or more.	(4)
Between three and six years.	(3)
Within the next three years.	(2)
Within the next six months.	(1)

What percent of my investable assets (not including house) does this investment represent?

Less than 25%	(4)
Between 25% and 50%	(3)
Between 50% and 75%	(2)
Greater than 75%	(1)

CH-CH-CHANGES

Why does the net asset value of an open-end mutual fund change? Here are some reasons:

- Performance of the stock and bond markets
- Dividend distributions, such as the dividends paid on the stock that the fund holds
- Capital gains distributions, such as gains from the fund selling stock for a higher price than it paid for it
- Unrealized capital gains, such as the price increase of a stock the fund is holding
- Redemptions, which affect the number of shares available in the fund
- Deposits, which also affect the number of shares available

How do I expect my income will grow over the next five years?

My income will:

Grow quickly due to a new job or promotion.	(4)
Grow ahead of inflation.	(3)
Grow slowly or not at all.	(2) ✓
Decrease due to retirement or raising children.	(1)

Do I have emergency savings?

Yes.	(4) ✓
Yes, but less than I'd like.	(3)
No.	(1)

I would feel comfortable risking ________ percent of my investable money if the chance of doubling it was ________ percent.

10% and 10%	(4)
25% and 25%	(3)
50% and 50%	(2) ✓
0% and 0%	(1)

Have I ever invested in individual stocks or stock mutual funds before?

Yes, and I was comfortable with it.	(4) ✓
No, but I look forward to it.	(3)
Yes, but I was uneasy with it.	(2)
No, and I don't want to.	(0)

What do I want my money to do for me?

Grow as fast as possible; current income not important.	(4) ✓
Grow faster than inflation; produce some income.	(3)
Grow slowly and provide a nice income.	(2)
Preserve principal, no matter what.	(1)

Add up your points. If your score was:

5	**You're a very conservative investor; stick with bank CDs.**
10	**You're a conservative investor; invest in funds that are 10 to 25 percent stock.**
15	**You're a moderate investor; invest in funds that are 25 to 50 percent stock.**
20	**You're an average investor; invest in funds that are 50 to 75 percent stock.**
25	**You're an aggressive investor; invest in funds that are 75 to 100 percent stock.**
30	**You're very aggressive; invest in 100 percent stock, international, and real estate funds.**

Regardless of your risk tolerance, you should try to diversify your investments among funds with different risks. Here are some rules of thumb for mixing and matching funds based on risk. We'll explain each in greater depth later.

- Very aggressive investors should keep 28 percent of their investments in money funds and 72 percent in aggressive growth, small-company stock, and growth stock mutual funds.

- Aggressive investors should keep 33 percent of their investments in money funds and 67 percent in aggressive growth, small-company stock, and growth stock mutual funds.

- Conservative investors who want some growth should keep 28 percent of their investments in money funds and 72 percent in growth-and-income funds.

- Very conservative investors who want some income should put 35 percent of their investments into money funds and 65 percent into high-dividend-yielding stock funds or growth-and-income funds.

KNOW *your* mutual FUND

CHAPTER FOUR

There** are two* ***classes *of mutual funds and you need to be able to tell them* ***apart****. The difference is in the number of shares that are for sale. Players who are new to this game should stick with open-end funds. Closed-end funds are for more experienced* ***investors.***

It's up to the investment company to decide whether it wants to offer open-end funds or closed-end funds—but there aren't many companies that do both. By and large, you're only going to be interested in open-end funds, but you should know the distinction between these classes of funds so you can find them in the right spot of your newspaper. (While it's easy to find the listings for the open-end funds in almost any daily newspaper, listings of closed-end funds are less common.)

The Two Compared

Closed-end funds have a fixed number of outstanding shares, like those that are sold by a public corporation, while open-end funds have an unlimited amount. Because open-end funds make up the majority of funds on the market today, when we refer to funds in this book, we are talking about open-end funds.

Open-end funds have shares available for sale at all times and will sell as many shares as investors will buy. There are some open-end funds that close their sales to new investors, but they always remain open to everyone who is already inside the tent when they "close" the fund. So existing investors can continue to buy shares, but no shares are sold to new investors.

Open-end funds will also buy back shares whenever an investor wants to redeem them. It will redeem them for the net asset value (NAV) of the shares at the close of the stock market on the day the redemption was requested. (Some funds will redeem shares based on the NAV at the close of the nearest business hour.)

The good thing about an open-end fund compared to a closed-end fund is you never have to worry about finding someone to buy your shares. The fund always has to buy the shares back from you. However, shares in an open-end fund can't be traded on the market. You can only buy and sell shares through the mutual fund company that issued them.

Known as quirky and so overlooked that they've been labeled "orphan" investment vehicles, closed-end funds were, until the 1929 crash, the chief type of publicly owned investments in the country. By the 1960s there were only about 60 closed-end funds, with $8 billion in assets. But during the 1980s and 1990s, their popularity picked up.

The shares of closed-end funds are publicly traded on an exchange or over-the-counter, like corporation shares. That's why you won't find them listed with the rest of the mutual funds in a newspaper. They're listed in the stock tables for the exchange on which they're traded.

Closed-end funds are similar to open-end funds in three ways:

1. Professional managers oversee your investment.

Closed-End Fund versus Open-End Fund

	Closed-End	Open-End
Diversification	Yes	Yes
Professional Management	Yes	Yes
Economies of Scale	Yes	Yes
Purchase/Sale	Broker, bank	Broker, direct
Shares	Fixed	Unlimited
Share Worth Determined By	The market	The fund's assets

2. They offer diversification for your portfolio.

3. They take advantage of the economies of scale, or the cost savings, that can be achieved by buying and selling securities in large quantities.

The difference is closed-end funds have several advantages over open-end funds because, theoretically, they have more opportunity to maximize their investors' returns by:

- Protecting investment decisions
- Increasing investment opportunities
- Leveraging funds

Here's why.

Protecting Investment Decisions

The open-end structure of mutual funds poses problems for the investment manager who is continually faced with money coming into the fund through the issuance of new shares and out of the fund through redemptions. All the money entering the fund has to be invested in assets that become part of the fund's portfolio. All money leaving the fund is paid by selling assets. There's a direct relationship between the fund's assets and its shares that doesn't exist in a closed-end fund. This fact of life forces an open-end fund manager's hand during periods of wild sentiment swings in the market.

At market tops, individual investors tend to pour money into funds, leaving the fund manager with the unpalatable choice of increasing cash positions or buying stocks at rich valuations. The first option, increasing cash positions, means putting money into investments with low yield. The other, buying stocks at rich valuations, means buying stocks at inflated prices. That means that the manager can't get the most yield for investment dollar from the purchase.

At market bottoms, individual investors tend to pull money from the funds, forcing the manager to sell stocks at low prices or to commit a larger portion of funds to cash

Interesting Developments

Just as stock funds are sensitive to the ups and downs of the marketplace, bonds are sensitive to changes in interest rates.

The length of time for which a bond is issued determines the impact a change in interest rates will have on your investment.

For instance, if you have $1,000 invested in a short-term bond and interest rates increase 1 percent, your investment drops in value 3.8 percent to $962. On the other hand, if interest rates drop 1 percent, your investment increases in value 4 percent to $1,040. If you invested that $1,000 in intermediate-term bonds, a 1 percent jump in interest rates would lower the value of your investment 6.2 percent to $938. A corresponding drop would increase the value of your investment 6.7 percent to $1,067. And if you had invested the $1,000 in long-term bonds? Your investment would have slipped 9.4 percent to $906 with a 1 percent interest rate hike; and climbed 11.2 percent to $1,112 with a 1 percent decline.

So rising interest rates are good for bond investors, right? Wrong! Keep in mind that rising interest rates are a sign of rising inflation, which eats into the worth of your principal. You get more income with higher interest rates, but you are able to buy less with it. Low interest rates may reduce your income, but the corresponding low inflation rate means you'll be able to buy more with the income you do receive.

as a cushion against such redemption. The closed-end fund manager doesn't have to worry about redemptions. When shareholders get antsy, they sell their stock and the price per share drops, but the fund manager doesn't have to take losses on assets to accommodate the trend.

Look at it this way. When stock prices boom, you invest $1,000 in an open-end fund. The fund issues you $1,000 worth of shares. Those shares represent assets in the fund. But if the fund doesn't have any assets for that $1,000 when it buys them back, it must acquire some—even if market conditions suggest it shouldn't.

If you were to buy $1,000 of a closed-end fund during the same period, the price of the shares would be dictated by the market, not by the worth of the assets in the fund (although, theoretically, the quality of those assets in the minds of investors determine the share price). The closed-end fund doesn't have to buy assets with your $1,000; in fact, it doesn't even see your $1,000. The fund manager has the latitude to wait and make his move when he wants to, not when he has to.

The open-end structure of mutual funds tends to push managers into bad decisions: buy at highs, sell at lows, or stay uninvested. In closed-end funds, the investment manager can make investment decisions uninfluenced by the erratic behavior of individual investors.

GENTLEMEN PREFER BONDS

A bond salesperson on Wall Street runs into an old high school chum. The pair catches up on old times and as they bid their adieus, the bond salesperson tells his friend: "If you see my folks, whatever you do, don't tell them what I do. I told them I was **playing piano** in a whorehouse."

But seriously, a few key individuals have managed to entertain us highly, while giving the entire bond sales profession a tainted image. For instance, Junk Bond King Michael Milken of Drexel Burnham used his groundbreaking antics of using junk bonds—a term applied to bonds with ratings of BB or lower—to finance corporate takeovers. **Milken** was a master at taking a very small amount of cash and leveraging it into a very large amount of money—a fact not lost on Wall Street wags when Milken's buddy Ivan Boesky got hit with a $100 million fine for insider training.

Increasing Investment Opportunities

The closed-end format facilitates investments in risky securities or markets. Often, many of the most profitable investments tend to be in companies that are at very early stages of growth, coming out of bankruptcy reorganization, or in emerging markets in developing countries. However, you can't bolt from those investments. You need to have a degree of patience to hang in there until the company starts to expand or turn itself around. Open-end funds tend to make those kinds of investments sparingly, since there is a danger that investors will panic during adverse market conditions and, through redemptions, force the sale of assets at temporarily depressed prices. Closed-end funds, however, since they do not have to worry about such redemptions, can make more lucrative investments and take more chances. Some invest in private placements, some invest in extremely small companies, some invest in thinly traded markets, and some invest in highly volatile securities like warrants. Closed-end funds offer higher growth and pose a greater risk, but they don't outperform open-end funds.

Leveraging Funds

A particularly bullish investment adviser may borrow additional funds to invest. Lenders are more comfortable making loans to closed-end funds since they have stable pools of investment money. Open-end funds have a much harder time borrowing money and leveraging since their capital pools may change rapidly and dramatically.

Let's Make a Trade

Since closed-end funds are traded on the floor of the stock exchange where they're listed, you need the services of a stockbroker to buy or sell them. You have to ante up to enter the fund and pay a commission to cash out, like you do when you invest in load funds. With the advent of deep-discount brokers, commissions are not as significant as before, however. Many brokerages offer excellent terms for the small investor:

- Flat fees ranging from about $18 to $30 for up to 5,000 shares.
- On a transaction of 5,000 shares of a typical closed-end fund with a price of $10, the costs are minuscule—0.12 percent ($60/$50,000).

- On a transaction of 1,000 shares of a $10 fund, the costs are small—0.6 percent ($60/$10,000).

- On a transaction of 200 shares of a $10 fund, the costs are comparable to a low-load fund—3 percent ($60/$2,000).

Investors who buy and sell a very small number of shares, however, may be better off with no-load mutual funds, since the commissions will represent a larger fraction of their investment.

How Are Prices Determined?

The share price of closed-end funds are determined by the market. That means a share's net asset value doesn't always jibe with the price at which the share is selling on a particular day. If investors feel a fund is undervalued, then the share price may be higher than the NAV. If investors feel a fund is overvalued, then the share price may be lower than the NAV.

For example, the NAV for a closed-end fund might be $49.77, but its share price may only be $40. That means you could buy a share of that fund for 19.62 percent less than its net asset value, which is a pretty nice deal. But the fact that the fund is so heavily discounted indicates investors are sour on the fund and they don't expect its future performance to be very good.

DOW MOMENTS

May 19, 1993—Dow breaks the 3,500 barrier (3,500.03).

Feb. 23, 1995—Dow crosses the 4,000 level (4,003.33).

On the other hand, another closed-end fund might have a NAV of $9.50 with its shares selling at $12.75. Investors apparently think the prospects for this fund are rosy. If you think so, too, though, you'll have to pay 34.19 percent more than the net asset value of the fund to join the party.

The truth of the matter, however, is that most closed-end funds trade at a discount or below their NAV. One index of closed-end funds showed a discount of near zero in early 1993, but within two years it had widened to the neighborhood of 12 percent, not far from the 15 percent level it reached just after the market crash in 1987. This apparently puts off many investors, although risk takers may find the situation to their liking. If you can follow a strategy of buying closed-ends when discounts are large and selling when they shrink to near zero or turn into premiums—when their stock price trades above their NAV—then you can turn a tidy profit.

However, before your eyes start spinning like slot machine dials with dollar signs instead of fruit, heed this caution: Getting mixed up with these funds isn't a good idea for a novice—or for anyone with an aversion to risk.

By and large, a good open-end fund will be better than a good closed-end fund. Why? Here are just a few reasons.

- *Economies of scale.* Because the tap is always open at an open-end fund, it can attract more money than a closed-end fund. Because these funds have more money, the managers of open-end funds have greater earning potential than managers of closed-end funds. This tends to attract more talent to the open-end funds. That's not to say there aren't talented closed-end managers; there's just more talent being attracted to the open-end funds.

- *Lower costs.* It's the old size argument again. Open-end funds can attract more money than closed-end funds. The more money that a fund can attract, the lower its expenses will be as a percentage of the fund's total assets. If the cost of running Open Fund A and Closed Fund B is the same (say $500,000), and Open Fund A has $1 billion in assets while Open Fund B has $500 million in assets, then, as a percentage of assets, the open fund's expenses (.05 percent) will be lower than the closed fund's (.1 percent). Since a fund's expenses are taken off the top of a fund's returns before the returns reach you, high expenses mean less money for you.

  Also, you can only buy closed-end funds through a broker. And since shares in closed-end funds are traded as stock, the commissions you must pay the broker to buy the shares tend to be higher than even the loads in open-end funds.

- *What you see is what you get.* With an open-end fund, the worth of the total shares outstanding is always equal to the total worth of the assets in the fund. That means you know exactly what your shares are worth. If you want to cash in your shares, you go to the fund, redeem them (the fund must take them back), and collect your money. With a closed-end fund, the price of your shares is detached from the assets of the fund. What your shares may be selling for on the market won't be equal to their asset value. Their price could be more, but more often than not, it's less. Moreover, if you want to sell your shares, you have to find a buyer for them—there isn't any nice open-end fund that has to take the shares back. If you can't find a buyer at one price, then you'll have to accept less for your shares, regardless of what their real worth may be, based on the value of the assets in the closed-end fund. So you see how much more complicated your situation gets with a closed-end fund.

What Affects NAV?

All the buying and selling activity of open-end funds affects the number of outstanding shares in the fund and the value of each of those shares. When someone buys shares, the fund has more capital with which to buy securities. That can affect the NAV. When someone cashes out of the fund, it has less money to invest in securities. And that will affect the NAV, too. So the NAV of a fund can change from day to day.

The securities within the fund will also fluctuate from day to day. Stocks go up, stocks go down, as the old saw goes. Bond prices move. All these changes will affect the NAV on any given day.

Funds maintain a large cash reserve to handle redemptions. But if investors make a run on a fund—as they did after the crash in 1987—the fund may have to ditch some of its holdings to meet the demand. This, too, can have an impact on the NAV.

Distributions will also affect a fund's NAV. One day, you might see a sudden drop in your fund's NAV even though the market was a raging bull that day. There may be a simple answer to this. The fund may have made a distribution. Or it may be doling out dividends its stocks earned or capital gains the fund made.

Scoping Out a Money Market Fund

Money market mutual funds are listed separately in the newspaper. When you find the listing, here's what those tiny numbers mean.

Fund	Avg Mat.	7 Day Yld.	Assets
FidelCal TaxFR	38	4.51	559.7

The first column is the fund name. In this case, it's the Fidelity Tax-Free Fund. Never would have guessed it, would you? Once you buy a fund, though, you'll be surprised at how quickly you catch on to that cryptic foreshortening of a fund's name.The second column tells you the average maturity of the securities in the fund. Here, the average holding matures in 38 days.

The third column shows the average interest rate on the outstanding loans in the portfolio. The last column shows you how much money is in the fund, in millions.

When a distribution is made, the temptation is to take the money and run. For example, if your fund makes a distribution of 50 cents a share and you have 1,000 shares, that $500 might look tempting to you. Try to resist. Reinvest the money instead. Here's why:

On the distribution date, the NAV for the fund will drop by 50 cents. If it was selling for $9.00 a share, it will fall to $8.50. You haven't lost any money, though, because you still have the dividend money. But now you can buy more shares of the fund at the discounted price of $8.50—a bargain you shouldn't pass up.

FUNDS *by* many a NAME

CHAPTER FIVE

Through the years, the brain trusts at the ***numerous*** *investment companies have worked overtime to exploit every angle they can think of for creating a fund. That's why you have so many funds from which to* ***choose.***

At one time, mutual funds were just broad-based investment instruments to enable small investors to capitalize on strategies (like diversification) and talent (like professional managers) that they wouldn't have access to if they were investing alone. Today, mutual funds incorporate a wide variety of investment styles and approaches.

Two terms you'll be hammered with over and over again as you review the many kinds of fund options are growth and income. Growth is used in connection with stocks. A stock can grow in two ways: Its stock price can increase, which is a function of the market, and its earnings can climb. Earnings represent a company's profits. The larger its profits, the larger the earnings it can pass on to its stockholders. That doesn't mean the company will pass the profits on in the form of earnings. It may sink the money back into the company to grow it—to develop new products, build new facilities, or hire new people.

Income is used in connection with both stocks and bonds. You can get income from a stock's earnings. You can get it from a stock's dividends, which is sort of an added bonus a company passes on to its stockholders. You can also get income from interest earned on bonds. How a fund mixes its appetite for growth and income is determined by its objectives.

Mutual Funds Offer Diversity

As most businesses do when they grow, mutual funds have become specialized. In the process, the diversity of funds available to the investor has become enormous. Portfolios run the investment spectrum. There's something for conservative investors, for aggressive investors, and all the investors in between. You can invest in funds that are primarily tied up in stocks, funds tied up in bonds, or funds that mix both kinds of securities. There are funds that invest in exclusively domestic companies and funds that only buy securities in foreign firms. You can sink your dough into taxable funds or nontaxable funds, into almost no-risk or high-risk funds.

What this diversity of offerings does for you is enable you to find just the right fund or group of funds to meet your investment objectives and goals. Let's look a little closer at the kinds of funds available to you. We'll start with the lowest-risk funds and work our way up to funds with higher risks. Finally, we'll look at tax-free funds.

Money Markets: Almost Like Taking Your Money to the Bank

A money market fund is probably the easiest to understand for the investment novice. It's a good place to start this discussion of fund types for several reasons. It's the most conservative type of fund you can invest in. And almost every investment company offers them.

If you want the principal you invest in a fund to be stable, if you want the power to get your hands on your money whenever you want it, and check-writing privileges and earnings that are as high or higher than certificates of deposit issued by banks (without the penalties for early withdrawal), then money market funds are for you.

Why Are They So Safe?

Money market funds were cooked up in the early 1970s, but they didn't catch on immediately. By 1977, there was only about $4 billion in assets in them. But when interest rates began to rise, largely due to sledgehammer inflation, it became apparent to investors that they could get better returns from these funds than they could from bank accounts. At the time, banks were limited to 5 percent interest—while money market funds were paying 15 to 16 percent interest on their accounts. By the early 1980s, investments in these funds had mushroomed to $200 billion.

Money market funds trade in very short-term debt. They lend money for short periods of time to companies and government bodies that pay it back with interest. It's called the "money market" because since these securities can be converted into cash so quickly, it's like holding money. By contrast, stocks and bonds, which are considered longer-term securities, trade in the capital market, that is, the wild and crazy market at large.

What do money market funds invest in? Some of their most common investments are:

- Commercial paper, which are short-term loans to corporations.
- Certificates of deposit, which are issued by large banks with maturities ranging from one month to several years. These include Eurodollar CDs issued by U.S. banks overseas and Yankee dollar CDs, issued by foreign banks in the United States.
- Bankers acceptance, which are short-term loans to importers and exporters. The loans are secured by the goods to be imported or exported.
- Short-term loans to municipalities and government agencies.
- Repurchase agreements, which are generally overnight loans to banks secured by U.S. Treasury securities.

Name That Goal

Whatever your investment goal, there is a product to meet it. Don't be afraid to mix and match fund types in your portfolio.

Goal	Kind of Fund	Potential Price Rise	Potential Current Income	Safety Level
Maximum Price Rise	*Aggressive Growth* Invests in common stock of fledgling companies and industries, out-of-favor companies, and industries.	Very High	Very Low	Low to Very Low
High Capital Gains	*Growth* Invests in the common stock of mature companies.	High to Very High	Very Low	Low
Price Rise and Current Income	*Growth and Income* Invests in companies with solid track records and consistent dividend payments.	Moderate	Moderate	Low to Moderate

Goal	Kind of Fund	Potential Price Rise	Potential Current Income	Safety Level
High Current Income	*Income* Invests in high-yielding stocks and bonds.	Very Low	High to Very High	Low to Moderate
Current Income and Maximum Safety	*Money Market* Invests in short-term debt securities.	None	Moderate to High	Very High
Current Income, Long-Term	*Balanced* Invests in mixture of bonds, preferred growth and safety stock, and common stock.	Low	Moderate to High	High
Tax-Free Income and Safety	*Tax-Free Money Market* Invests in short-term municipal notes and bonds.	None	Moderate to High	Very High
Tax-Free Income and Safety	*Municipal Bond* Invests in bonds exempt from state, local, and federal taxes.	Low to Moderate	Moderate	Moderate to High

- Treasury bills, which are issued by the federal government and mature in 30 to 90 days.

Although these investments are about as safe as you can get, the Securities and Exchange Commission, which regulates the mutual fund industry, has imposed a few rules on these kinds of investments to make them as bulletproof as possible.

- A minimum of 95 percent of a money market fund's assets must be invested in securities top rated ("junk bonds," also known as "high-yield" bonds need not apply) by Standard & Poor's and Moody's. Top-rated commercial paper carries an A1 rating from Standard & Poor's and P1 from Moody's.

- No more than 1 percent of a money market fund's assets may be invested in the securities of any one issuer whose rating is below the top rating.

- No more than 5 percent of a fund's assets can be invested in any one issuer except for obligations to the U.S. government. (Fund managers usually play it safer than that. They ordinarily don't invest more than 2 or 3 percent of their assets in any one issuer. That way, if the investment goes sour, it won't hurt the overall performance of the fund.)

- The maximum maturity period for any fund's holdings is 90 days. That means the fund's assets are not tied up for longer than three months in any particular investment. The less time a fund holds a company's paper, the less time there is for something to go wrong. There's less risk a lender will default on a loan that runs for 30 days than a loan that runs for 30 years.

- Limitations have also been placed on the purchase of derivatives, a complex security that is used to hedge risk but which can hammer its owners if interest rates swing up abruptly.

Are They Stable?

Money market funds are so stable that they can maintain a fixed-share price of $1. That means if you buy 100 shares at a dollar a share, those 100 shares are going to be worth $100 today, tomorrow, next year. There's no yo-yo factor.

The share price of some funds have dipped below $1 from time to time, but when that happens, managers will quickly dig deep into the fund's cash to brace up the price of its shares. They can keep the NAV at $1 because the underlying securities almost never lose their value. These managers realize that letting the price of their fund's shares drop below $1 not only jeopardizes confidence in their funds but in all money market funds.

The fund makes money for you by collecting interest on the money it lends to companies and governments. Governments and companies don't default on six-month loans. The trade-off is yield. You might get a 4 percent return on a money market fund while you could be making between 8 and 10 percent with a stock and bond fund. How much your money earns from day to day varies as the term on one loan in the portfolio runs out and a new loan is made. The interest rate on the expired loan could be higher or lower than the rate on the new loan depending on market conditions.

Nevertheless, your principal remains intact. Money market funds have several advantages over bank savings accounts:

- They are almost as secure but return a higher interest rate and therefore make more for you on your investment.

LOOK BEFORE YOU LEAP

Before you invest in an aggressive growth fund, it's wise to take some time to scrutinize the fund's performance. Check for **consistent returns.** Then look to see how it performed in the slump years of 1981, 1984, 1987, and 1990. You don't want a fund that does so poorly in a bad year that it negates the gains it makes in the good years.

Next, check the fund's expenses. The lower the ratio, the more money you'll earn. If you're going to assume the kinds of risks inherent in these funds, you want to make the **most money** you can. Small is better here—funds with assets under $200 million have more flexibility in this area than billion-dollar funds. Finally, check the median capitalization of the companies in the fund. Companies under $500 million in capitalization have greater risks, but they also have more pop in their punch.

- They come in taxable and nontaxable forms—it's your choice. Bank accounts are always taxable.

- They let you write checks on them—although the checks are limited to large amounts and take longer to clear than checks written on a bank checking account. So you still have the convenience of being able to draw on your money, while earning a higher interest rate than a typical checking account.

- They give you a launching pad to purchase shares in other funds within the sponsor's family of funds. It's a safe place for you to keep money that can be transferred easily to the other, higher interest-bearing funds when they do well.

A money market fund is about as safe an investment as you can make without having the Federal Deposit Insurance Corporation insure your principal (although investment companies are tinkering with the insurance idea for money market accounts). There's almost no downside to them. Well, there is one downside: You might be able to make more money by investing in another type of fund. Money market funds tend to have lower yields and lower total returns than other kinds of riskier investments.

Income Funds: Sidling Up to the Cash Bar

When you're willing to take on more risk but would still like to concentrate on accumulating income, with growth as a secondary concern, then you should consider income funds.

These funds are skewed toward accumulating income and preserving capital. The risk in the funds goes up as a manager tries to maximize yields. So if the manager sticks close to money market–type investments—short-term loans, blue-chip corporate stocks, government securities—the risk will remain low. If the manager starts to venture into investments such as long-term bonds and high-yield bonds (aka junk bonds), then the fund's risk increases.

Investors in income funds may aim for one or more of the following goals:

- Seek to make current income higher than money market rates for people who are willing to accept moderate price fluctuations.
- Balance their stock portfolios with a mixed income investment.
- Create a portfolio of taxable bonds with differing maturity dates.
- Obtain periodic income on a regular business.

Income funds are suitable for investors living on fixed incomes who are looking for investments with better returns than what they can get with certificates of deposit or money market funds. The funds have consistently outperformed the S & P 500—a popular measure of investment performance—and outdistanced inflation. From 1984 to 1994, for example, inflation increased at an average annual rate of 3.8 percent. During that same period, income funds grew at a rate of 13.3 percent, or 9.5 percent over income.

That kind of return makes an income fund a good investment if you intend to make systematic withdrawals as income. If you withdrew 5 percent a year, the fund would still be growing by 4.5 percent and keeping pace with inflation.

Income funds usually invest more of their assets in bonds than stocks, because bonds produce more fixed income than stocks. The stocks the funds do hold tend to pay high dividends—utilities and natural resources, financial services and nondurable goods companies.

Income funds have shown good performance over the last 20 years or so, but they're not without risks. When interest rates rise, their value may decline because the funds invest in interest-sensitive stocks and bonds. A stock market tumble may also pull down the value of a fund. During bullish times, income funds may not perform as well as other types of stock funds, but over the long term they're solid performers.

The Bond That Tithes

Another type of mutual fund that zeroes in on income is the bond fund. Unlike the income fund that will mix its portfolio with stocks and bonds, the bond fund deals strictly in bonds.

Money market funds and bond funds account for about two-thirds of all the assets in mutual funds. Both will generate income for you with considerably less risk than a mutual fund that is trading in stock.

Bond funds are riskier than money market funds so if you can't stand to see any kind of fluctuation in an original investment, stay away from these funds. As always, the additional risk connected with these funds means the potential for greater income and earnings is better over the long term.

Like income funds, bond funds are good investment vehicles for investors with fixed incomes. Retirees find the monthly income allocations from the funds particularly attractive. Bond funds are also good vehicles for diversifying your mutual fund investments because their values often shift in the opposite direction of changes in stock value. So if your stock mutual fund takes a wrong turn, your bond fund can help cover your financial fundament.

Bond Terms

You can limit some of the risk tied to bond funds by investing in a fund that stakes out the middle ground between money market–type investments and riskier long-term bonds. These short-term bond funds can earn you as much as 1 percent more over money market accounts. Short-term bond funds invest in loans with slightly longer maturities—three years or so—compared with the typical 90-day maturity of money market funds.

Another strategy is to invest in bond funds that only buy highly rated bonds (ratings of A to AAA). Although a bit riskier than the short-term route, the reward is that much greater.

Here are some sample bond ratings:

Standard & Poor's	Moody's	Translation
AAA	Aaa	Highest quality. True gilt-edged bonds.
AA	Aa	High quality but slightly more risky than a triple A bond.
A	A	Strong, but issuers lack

Standard & Poor's	Moody's	Translation
		financial muscle of higher rated bonds.
BBB	Baa	Medium-grade bonds. Short-term outlook is good, but might be risky in the long run.
BB to B	Ba to B	Speculative bonds. Risk of getting stiffed is high. Junk bonds begin in this category.
CCC to C	Caa to C	You're in the red zone on the risk meter.
D		Take a trip to the track.

Bond funds fall into three categories, which are defined by the length of time it takes for the purchaser to be repaid:

1. Short-term. The bond matures after two years.
2. Intermediate-term. The bond matures after seven years.
3. Long-term. The bond matures after 20 years.

Remember, the longer it takes for a bond to mature, the greater the risk connected to the bond and the greater the yield to the investor. That's because the longer a debt is outstanding, the wider the window opens for something bad to happen.

Bond Types

Once you've decided the length of the term, you must also condsider the type of bond that the fund will invest in. Here are the major tax-free players:

- *Treasuries.* These are issued by Uncle Sam. There are Treasury bills, which mature in 13, 26, or 52 weeks; Treasury notes, which mature in one to ten years; and Treasury bonds, which mature in more than ten years. Interest from Treasuries can't be taxed by the state, but are taxed by the feds, a nice trick that all bond issuers wish they had the power to do.

- *Municipals.* These bonds are issued by state and local governments. Their income is free from federal tax and from local taxes—if you live in the state that issued the bonds. But the issuers of these bonds know the score and issue their bonds at lower than the prevailing rates.

- *Corporates.* Corporations issue these bonds. There's no free lunch on their income. It's all taxable.

- *Mortgages.* Government agencies such as the Government National Mortgage Association (Ginnie Mae) and the Federal National Mortgage Association (Fannie Mae) raise the money they lend in the form of mortgages through bonds. The bonds are purchased by investors. Investors don't have to worry about losing their principal on these loans because the federal government backs them with its credit. If a mortgage turns to vinegar, the feds will sweeten the taste by paying off the loan from the U.S. Treasury.

- *Convertibles.* These bonds are cross-dressers. They walk and talk like bonds, but can be converted into the common stock of the company that issued them. The interest rate is lower than other bonds, but they might bring you bigger gains if the underlying stock increases in value because the trading price of the bond is closely tied to the price of that stock. The terms of exchange are set when the bond is issued. The bondholder can decide whether or not to convert the bond to common stock as the bond approaches maturity.

- *International bonds.* Foreign governments and corporations all issue bonds and anyone can buy them. If you do, you can worry not only about defaults and interest rate changes, but about currency fluctuations, too.

As we mentioned before, mutual funds that buy government bonds can be used to shelter the fund's income from taxes. The formula for determining whether one of these bond funds makes sense for you is a simple one. Take the yield of the prospective tax-free bond fund and divide it by the result of 100 minus your federal tax bracket. So if the target tax-free fund yields 6 percent and your tax bracket is 31 percent, a taxable fund would have to earn 6 divided by 69 (100 minus 31) or 8.7 percent to equal the yield of a tax-free fund.

Growth and Income Funds: Chips Off the Blue Block

Growth and income funds aim for long-term growth of principal while delivering reasonable current income. They do that by investing in stocks with growth potential that still pay market or above-market dividend income.

These funds invest in blue-chip companies with track records for paying dividends. These companies show growing profits more often than not, and they pass about 50 to 60 percent of it on to their shareholders through dividends.

But the managers of these funds also look for capital appreciation, so they want to see earnings growth, too. This means they'll buy the stock of large companies that are expected to show better earnings than their peers or stock that is undervalued.

Some companies that have fit this bill in the past are Philip Morris, General Electric, Merck, Exxon, and AT&T.

Risks are moderate because these companies have the cash flow to pay big dividends and cushion any market fluctuations. There's some volatility, but much less than you'd see in a pure growth fund. Over a recent ten-year period, growth and income funds hit a high return of 19.4 percent and a low of minus 1.0 percent. Compare that with 23.8 percent and minus 11.3 percent for growth funds during the same period and you can see what we mean.

If you want some growth and moderate income over the long term (five years or more), these are your funds.

Balanced Funds: A Balancing Act

The objective of balanced funds is similar to that of growth and income funds: generate income and long-term growth of principal. These funds invest in common and preferred stocks and bonds. In fact, these funds bridge the gap between stock and bonds funds. Usually the holdings of these funds are 60 percent blue chip and 40 percent U.S. government and high-grade corporate bonds. Some managers may try to juice their fund's performance by investing 10 to 15 percent of its assets in small company and foreign stocks with good growth potential. Or they may buy lower-grade junk bonds to bolster the fund's yields.

Their price rise potential is low but they have moderate to high income potential. Overall, balanced funds make about 80 percent of what a stock fund makes. The funds are less risky than stock funds but a little more risky than some bond funds. They tend to lose 50 percent less than stock funds when things go badly, so when a stock fund loses 10 percent of its value, chances are a balanced fund will lose only 5 percent. While they'll lag behind stock funds during a bull market, they'll outperform the market during bear periods.

A variation of the balanced fund is the asset allocation or total return fund. With these funds, managers try to outguess the market. They'll tinker with the stock-bond mix of the fund based on how they believe the market will do or where interest rates will go. Usually these funds don't do as well as funds that stay invested in good stocks and bonds, which stay away from trying to time the market.

A word of warning about balanced funds. Because the bond portion of the portfolio pays some good-sized dividends, these funds may not be good for investors in the higher federal tax brackets—31 percent and over. However, there are balanced funds for these investors, too.

Growth Funds: The Principal's the Thing

Growth funds aim to make your capital grow over the long term. When you see the word "growth," it means the fund is designed to take advantage of increases in the stock price of the issues it holds. It wants to buy a stock at a low price, then sell it after a decent run-up of the price.

LEADING LOAD FUND COMPANIES

AIM
Alliance
American
American Capital
Dean Witter
Franklin/Templeton
IDS
Kemper
Merrill Lynch
MFS (Massachusetts Financial Services)
Nuveen
Oppenheimer
PaineWebber
Prudential
Putnam
Smith Barney Shearson

A secondary goal is to grow your capital faster than inflation can eat it away. Historically, these funds have been good at managing to keep their yields about 7 percent above the rate of inflation.

Dividend income is an afterthought in these funds. They usually invest part of their assets in well-heeled companies that pay dividends, but dividend accumulation just isn't part of the game plan. And the yields for these vechicles—the dividends and interest paid to you by the fund—show it.

Growth funds are best suited for investors who want to grow their principal. These are considered long-term investments—lasting three to five years—so jumping in and out of these funds isn't advisable (although if your fund doesn't show substantial growth in three to five years, you should dump it and get another one).

Management styles in these funds vary. Some managers base their decision to include an issue in their funds primarily on expected earnings. Others base their decisions on the value of a stock. That essentially means they think they see something positive in the company that isn't reflected in its earnings performance past, present, or future.

What's that mean to you? A fund based on earnings momentum tends to have a shorter outlook on things than a value-based fund. Don't be surprised if all the stocks in an earnings-oriented fund turn over in a year. Value-based funds are looking at strong earnings growth over the long term and expect you to share their patience. In these funds, the manager may let certain stocks stick around for a year or two to give them the time they need to develop.

LEADING NO-LOAD FUND COMPANIES

Acorn
Columbia
Federated
Fidelity Investments
Harbor
Invesco
Janus
Mutual Series
Neuberger & Berman
Nichola
PIMCO
Charles Schwab
Scudder, Stevens & Clark
SteinRoe
Strong
T. Rowe Price
Twentieth Century–Benham
USAA
Vanguard
Warburg Pincus

Your temperament should be fairly aggressive to get into these funds since their stock and trade are moderate to risky investments.

Aggressive Growth: Risk Is Their Middle Name

When growth funds start shedding their blue chips, they start becoming aggressive growth funds, or capital appreciation funds. These funds are the riskiest of all the stock, or equity, funds. In these funds, income is sacrificed on the altar of capital appreciation.

Companies that are included in the fund's portfolio have a history or a potential for big movement in their stock prices. They don't pay dividends because they sink every penny they earn back into the company to finance growth.

New companies and existing growth companies on the over-the-counter market are favorites of these funds. So are companies that have fallen out of favor with investors, which may make them undervalued and good prospects for a price spurt. There are value headhunters in the aggressive fund crowd, too, so companies with lurking profit potential also catch the eye of managers of these funds.

Dubbed "go-go" funds in the 1960s, these mutuals can outperform the market as much as 25 percent to 30 percent, but they can underperform the market by just as much as well. A manager makes the wrong picks. The market takes a dive. And you can kiss a good portion of your investment good-bye.

During a 15-year period ending in May 1992, aggressive growth funds grew at an annual average rate of 15.4 percent. But there were some big dips in that run. In 1984, aggressive funds lost 12.9 percent. And in the crash of 1987, they lost 27 percent in one month.

If you balance your investments with more conservative funds, you can benefit from these funds and cushion your losses. You won't make as much as if you were 100 percent invested in an aggressive fund during an up market, but you can corral a good portion of that gain.

Most investment advisers recommend that only a small amount of your money—an amount you can afford to lose without pain—be funneled into aggressive growth funds.

Short-term losses may be unavoidable in these funds, but if you have the brass to stick it out over the long term—for ten years or more—you'll find these funds to be big gainers.

Index Funds: Automatic Systematic

As we mentioned before, there are certain market measures against which fund managers gauge their performance. They want to do better than the S & P 500 or the Dow Jones Industrial Average. That isn't easy to do. So index funds take a page out of chairman Alfred E. Neuman's rule book and say, "What? Me worry?" and simply set up their holdings based on the companies in the S & P 500 or the Dow. If the market goes up, the fund goes up; if the market stumbles, so do the funds.

One advantage of these funds is they don't need managers. They're more or less on automatic. That cuts down on the cost of running the funds. They don't need regiments of analysts, either, which also helps keep expenses low.

And while actively managed funds must buy and sell their holdings frequently to pump up their growth, index funds don't need to "churn" their holdings very much at all because they are based on a standard group of stocks. That saves you money, too. When a fund sells a stock and makes a capital gain, capital gains are distributed to the fund's investors. And they must pay capital gains taxes on these distributions. The more often these distributions are made, the more often you pay taxes. Since the holdings in an index fund stay relatively stable, there's fewer of these taxable distributions to worry about.

The fund simply buys the stocks on the index it's following—weighted the same way they are in the market indicator—and sits back and lets the market take its course.

Index funds don't get a lot of respect from fund insiders—which shouldn't be surprising. If an investment company pulls in millions of dollars from fees charged to manage a fund, it can't really claim to hold in very high regard a fund that is successful without intensive management. However, keep in mind that over ten years or more, these funds have performed better than three-quarters of the funds out there—which emphasizes the point that it isn't as easy to beat the S & P 500 and Dow as it might appear.

An index fund isn't going to outperform the market, but it won't underperform it by much either. And the fund's low expenses means a little more money in your pocket.

Sector Funds: Narrowband Investing

When mutual funds were invented, the idea behind them was to invest in a broad spectrum of securities to dilute risk and avoid placing too many eggs in one basket. Sector funds fly in the face of this idea. They do put all their eggs in one basket by selecting stocks from a specific sector of the marketplace—energy, technology, biotech, and the like.

There's a lot of risk in this approach and a lot of gain, too. In 1983, Fidelity Select Technology gained 52.5 percent. The next year it lost 16.9 percent. In 1985, it returned to the black and gained 7.5 percent. Then over the next three years it lost 29 percent.

During bear days, a sector fund can be used as a hedge against a down market. Sectors with companies that provide goods that have a stable demand in good times and bad—soap, food, electricity—are likely prospects. In fact, funds specializing in utilities are considered pretty safe investments. Income from the funds is good and you can expect your annual return to be around 10 percent or better regardless of what the economy does. When you invest in these funds, you need a savvy about what direction a sector is moving in—a savvy that even professionals don't always have.

Specialized Funds: Novices Need Not Apply

Specialized funds resemble sector funds. They lack diversification, but don't focus on industries. Rather, they select stocks from a very narrow slice of the market: initial public offerings, for example, or foreign securities.

Precious metal funds like gold funds fall into this category. Precious metal prices skyrocket when the prices of necessities such as food, clothing, and energy climb. That's why gold is seen as such a good hedge against inflation. During the energy crisis in the early 1970s, gold prices hit $800 an ounce and the price of gold stocks went up 100 percent. But with more stable times, the returns from gold funds have lagged behind the equity markets.

Real estate funds also fall into this category. A common method of investing in real estate by a mutual fund is to invest in REITs—Real Estate Investment Trusts. These trusts are packages of stocks of companies that invest in real estate.

Still another type of specialty fund worth mentioning is the socially responsible fund. These funds try to invest in companies that are "doing the right thing" and steer clear of companies that make products that are harmful to society. A socially responsible fund would steer clear of tobacco stocks and defense contractors, for example, and invest in companies that advance social justice.

Defining what's socially responsible and what isn't is very subjective and can be a real can of worms when trying to make predictions. That is probably why major fund sponsors such as Fidelity and Vanguard don't offer such funds. For example, one such fund invests in McDonald's because of the charitable work it does for children. On the other hand, if you consider what the company has done to the eating habits of society, it could be argued that this is not a socially responsible investment. One person's socially responsible company is another person's social reprobate. Like sector funds, these funds are for sophisticated investors. Novices should stay with more traditional funds.

International Funds: The Ultimate Game of Risk

International funds are composed of stocks and bonds of companies in overseas countries. There are broad-based funds encompassing companies in several countries. And there are funds targeted at companies in a particular region or an individual country. A so-called global fund will even mix some U.S. stocks with its foreign investments making it a true international fund. For most of us, understanding how our own economy works is hard enough, so figuring the ins and outs of a foreign one may be an overload for our economic acumen.

The benefit is that adding an international fund to your stock portfolio creates another level of diversity to your financial planning. The world markets don't all move in the same direction simultaneously, so chances are you can cover or cushion setbacks in the domestic market with gains in those overseas. International bond funds can do the same thing for you. For example, in 1987 T-bond funds lost almost 1 percent for the year while world bond funds gained 16 percent for the year.

The rule of thumb for evaluating the risk of an international fund is to find out how many countries are included in the portfolio. The more countries involved, the less risk it's taking on.

In addition, consider the stability of the countries included in an international fund. Some areas of the world have highly unstable governments—not the best of situations for an investor. For one, financial reporting standards aren't as stringent as they are here, making it easier for fund managers to stub their toes on some bad information. And currency fluctuations add a whole new dimension of risk for an overseas investor. If a country's currency declines against the dollar, the value of your fund may drop; if it increases in value against the dollar, the value of your fund may increase.

LOADS *and* loads *of* FUN

CHAPTER SIX

***Popular wisdom says that there are no* free *lunches. And that applies to mutual funds, too, because as advantageous as these investment vehicles are, you still have to pay for the* service.**

That said, you do have some choice about what you'll pay to participate in a fund. So although the lunch may not be free, you can still decide whether you want to eat at a restaurant with white tablecloths or one with take-out only.

Load versus No-Load

You'll feel the weight of a loaded fund when you're charged the current net asset value plus a sales commission. That commission is called a load. The load goes into the pocket of whoever sold you the shares of the fund, usually a broker. And it's the way the fund pays someone for selling its shares to you. Usually this person doesn't work for the sponsor of the fund but is an independent third party.

You don't have to buy into a load fund from a third party. You can go directly to the fund sponsor. But they'll collect a load anyway and it will go in their own pocket instead. Load charges have a wide spread. They can be as low as 2.5 percent of a total purchase or as high as 8.5 percent. The average is about 5 percent. Loads reduce the amount of money of your investment. If you invest $1,000 into a fund that charges a 2.5 percent load, you'll only have $975 working for you in the fund.

Types of Loads

If you pay a load when you buy your shares in a mutual fund, it's called a front-end load. Another kind of load, called a back-end load, is like a time bomb. If you redeem your shares within a certain period after purchasing them—say five or six years—you'll have to pay the load, which usually starts at 5 or 6 percent. If you stay invested in the fund beyond the specified time frame, you won't be charged the load when you cash out. Mutual funds are supposed to be long-term investments. Back-end loads give the fund sponsor a little insurance that the fund will be treated that way.

Yet another variation on the load theme is the level load. This load is around 1 percent. It usually includes a fee that many funds charge—the 12b-1 fee that pays for marketing and advertising a fund. It is capped at three-quarters of a percent by federal regulation and has an additional quarter percent service fee. Level loads are levied every year.

If you absolutely, positively must buy a load fund, you should decide how long you want to hold it before you pay the load. If you're confident you're going to hold the fund beyond the point when the back-end load expires, then that kind of makes sense. If you don't know how long you're going to hold the fund—and you can't find a no-load fund that suits your taste—then pay the front-end load. Many investors cash out of their funds in a panic, skittered by a sudden downturn in the market. With the worth of your shares going down, you don't want the worth of your assets further depleted by getting whacked with a back-end load. Just keep in mind, if you're paying a 1 percent annual load, over ten years that's the equivalent of a 10 percent front-end load.

No-Brainer

No-load funds sell their shares to you directly at net asset value. There's no middleman so there's no markup on the sale. If you invest $1,000 in a no-load fund, you have $1,000 working for you from day one.

It doesn't take a particle physicist to figure out that the best deal—especially for a novice investor—is to invest in a no-load fund. After all, what would you rather have working for you—100 percent of your investment or 90 percent?

The relationship between sales charges and performance has been studied ad nauseum. What's been discovered time and time again is that sales charges have—at best—no relationship at all to performance and—at worst—a negative relationship.

For example, if you invested $10,000 in a no-load fund and that fund had a 10 percent average return over 20 years, your account, that return, compounded over that period, would be worth $65,717. If you made the same investment for the same period of time in a fund with a load that performed at the same level, your investment would be worth $60,000 at the end of the period.

But maybe you don't need a deal. Maybe you need a broker. An investment professional can help you identify your objectives and measure your risk tolerance. He can identify the right funds for you from the thousands of funds out there. And he can analyze your tax situation and steer you toward funds that fit it. If you think you need those kinds of services, then the load you pay a broker may be worth it to you. On the other hand, if those things are important to you, you could hire a registered financial adviser, pay the fee, and ask her to find you a no-load fund or set of funds that meet your needs.

Paying the Piper

You may be able to keep your investment safe from loads by buying into a no-load fund, but there are other expenses that you won't be able to escape when you enter a fund. You don't write a check for these operating expenses every year. Indeed, they're pretty much invisible to you. But like the invisible hand of the marketplace, they do affect your return from the fund.

One operating expense is the management fee. This fee pays for the expenses of a fund—hiring people, research, and the cost of investing your cash. All funds charge them, even no-load funds. It's easy to find out what percentage of a fund's assets goes to management fees. It's spelled out in the fund's prospectus. We'll take apart prospectuses later. For now, rest easy knowing that you'll be able to figure out what the fees are before you invest.

Management fees are deducted from the total assets of the fund. Every day. So there's no way to time your exit from a fund to avoid their impact. The costs vary from fund to fund, but they are all listed in that good old prospectus.

The reason you should pay close attention to operating expenses is obvious. Operating expenses can amount to millions of dollars; that's millions that are subtracted from the total assets of the fund. That affects the value of your shares and the amount of your yield.

Evaluating Fees

You should try to select a fund with low expense ratios. The expense ratio shows how much the fund is deducting for expenses as a percentage of the fund's average net assets: 1 to 1.5 percent annually is a good number, half a percent is better.

Stock funds typically have higher expense ratios than bond funds; international funds have higher ratios than domestic funds. The average expense ratio for a stock fund is 1.2 percent; for a bond fund, .75 percent. That compares with 1.5 percent for an international stock fund and 1.13 percent for an international bond fund.

There are some finance types who would argue that "you get what you pay for." Funds with high operating expenses will perform better than funds with low expenses. But there's no evidence of that. More often than not, funds with high operating costs just return less to you—period.

Remember, if you pay 2 percent more for expenses in your fund than in a comparable fund, and both funds average a 12 percent total return over ten years, you've sacrificed 20 percent of your total return.

Although you can avoid an up-front sales charge when you initially buy your shares of a mutual fund by choosing a no-load fund, some funds—even no-loads—charge a redemption fee when you cash out of your fund. This fee is a percentage of the worth of the shares you redeem—usually about half a point, or one-half of 1 percent. That means if you redeem $1,000 in shares and a redemption fee of one-half a percentage point is imposed on that redemption, you'll receive $995.

Like the Ebola virus, redemption fees are to be avoided. The fees are another way mutual fund companies try to insure that investors won't "churn" their investments and skip from fund to fund as a butterfly flits from flower to flower in May. The fact is, you shouldn't be treating an investment in a fund as if it were an investment in a single stock. But if you do, that's your decision and you don't need a fund company telling you what to do with your money by penalizing you with redemption fees.

Another way a fund company gets a "taste" of a fund's assets is through the 12b-1 fee. Authorized in 1980, this fee allows a fund to charge an additional fee for the cost of marketing and distributing a fund. No-load funds rarely impose this fee.

Some mutual funds let you move your money among their family of funds. This practice is called switching. For many years, mutual funds allowed this practice for free. But as the industry ballooned and more speculative investors entered the market, the cost of switching grew. There are administra-

SUPERMARKET BROKERAGES

For years, the only way you could buy shares in a mutual fund was directly from the investment company that founded it. This created a number of problems for some investors. For one, you'd find yourself filling out a similar form over and over for different companies. Then, you'd receive a **separate statement** for each fund you own. And if you wanted to sell a fund from one company and buy one from another? You had to redeem your shares with the first company, wait for them to cut you a check, then set up an account with the second company.

Brokerages offer **one-stop shopping** (for a small fee of course). You open an account with the discount broker and buy and trade funds across companies. Moreover, you receive a single statement summarizing all your activity and, when tax time rolls around, you'll receive a single form 1099.

tive costs involved, and if it happens often, it could cost a fund some significant change. In response to that potential, some funds created a "switching fee"—a flat fee charged to your account every time you make a switch. This fee, as the other fees mentioned here, should be avoided, if possible. But if you're going to put your money in a fund and not be a wheeler-dealer, there's no reason to fret over this fee.

Another interesting fee to hit the scene recently is the maintenance fee. This fee is similar to the one banks charge for the privilege of giving them your money. The reason for these fees is to offset the cost of maintaining a customer's account. Usually pegged at about $10 a year, the fee is charged quarterly. So $2.50 is taken out of the dividends your account earns each quarter to pay this fee. If the fee can't be covered by your dividends, the money will be taken from the value of your shares. This appears to be a dubious fee, because it doesn't seem to have any impact on another fee—the one for accounting costs. In fact, it appears that companies charging the maintenance fee may be charging you for the same thing twice. When scrutinizing a prospectus, a red flag should go up when you see the words "maintenance fee."

All this talk of fees may be starting to make you feel uncomfortable. Don't be. After all, did the fee structure at a bank induce you to sock your cash in an argyle sock under your mattress? Even if you enter a fund without analyzing its fee structure, the chances are you're still going to get a good return on your money. But casting an arched eye on these expenses will help you earn even more.

TIPS *to help* the *greenhorn* PROFIT

CHAPTER SEVEN

W*ith all those costs and expenses associated with mutual funds, you might be* **wondering** *if there is a better way to invest. For a green investor, the answer is no. The positives definitely outweigh the* **negatives.**

You can't beat the advantages a mutual fund offers investment neophytes—unless you have millions of dollars to invest. Since most people don't have that kind of money lying around, mutual funds make sense for most people who want to build their wealth in a relatively safe way. And that's why more than half the households in America have invested in at least one mutual fund.

Diversify, Diversify, Diversify

It is rumored that one Wall Street tycoon once said that the only way to make a fortune in the market is to put all your eggs in one basket and then watch the hell out of the basket. As such stories do, the tale ends there and it remains to be discovered whether or not the tycoon remained a tycoon by employing that strategy or ended up on the Bowery. However, there are certainly less risky strategies you can employ as an investor.

The key to safe investing (although investing, like sex, is never totally without risk) is diversification. The more baskets in which you distribute your eggs, the less risk you expose yourself to.

By law, mutual funds must diversify their assets among a variety of security issuers. They may invest in 50 to 100 securities, far more than most investors have the wherewithal to invest in alone. Diversification provided by mutual funds offers the dual benefit of tempered volatility and potentially higher returns than singular investment options. It's important to understand that each type of investment (stocks, bonds, Treasury bills, sector funds) follows a market cycle all its own. Each responds differently to changes in the economy or in the investment marketplace.

For example, during the past decade, many foreign stock markets performed nearly as well as the U.S. stock market when their returns were translated into U.S. dollars. Foreign markets frequently move in different directions than the U.S. market (just as stocks and bonds move in opposite directions). So investors who owned a mix of both domestic and international stocks would have balanced the effects of changes in the stock market and reduced the overall volatility of their portfolios. When

DID WE MENTION DIVERSITY?

Risk reduction is best achieved by spreading your investment dollars in these ways.

- **By country,** so you don't have to depend on the stock market performance of any one country. For example, you might want to balance a fund that has most of its holdings in Europe with a fund that has holdings in Asia.

- **By industry,** preferably in different sectors of the marketplace (service and manufacturing, for example).

- **By company,** meaning your investment in airline companies should include different airlines in North America, Europe, Asia, and Australia.

- **By currency,** so you don't face the potential for significant losses as currencies change in value.

things were going well overseas, they frequently paled in the States. When the U.S. markets had cause to celebrate, the foreign markets often did not fare as well.

Compare the disparate results for international stocks (a 70 percent gain and a 23 percent loss) with the relatively stable results for money markets (an 8 percent gain and a 5 percent loss). Pretty convincing.

It is not only a good idea for a mutual fund to diversify its holdings, it's a good idea for you to diversify your mutual fund investments among several investment companies and among several funds with differing objectives. It's the only way to keep risk to a minimum and to earn attractive returns. That's true for your mutual fund manager and it's true for you.

Stay In for the Long Haul

In addition to diversifying, the only way to maximize your return over time without exposing your investment to undue risk is to stay invested. Many investors respond to market setbacks by heading for the bomb shelter, or pulling back their money into money market funds and certificates of deposit (CDs). As a short-term strategy, that may be okay, but in the long term, it isn't a good way to earn attractive returns.

Suppose all your money was invested in stocks and you needed to sell some of your holdings to make a down payment on a house. If stocks were depressed when you needed to sell, you could be forced to take a loss. Owning other investments would give you more flexibility in raising the necessary cash, allowing you to hold your stocks until prices improved.

Volatility is also hard on the nerves. Even if you do not have a pressing need for money, sizable price changes might tempt you to sell an investment at just the wrong time. Those diversified funds will allow you to stay invested in the market during good times and bad.

If greater stability is the goal, why not invest exclusively in money market securities? You could do that, but there are drawbacks. While money market instruments such as Treasury bills provide liquidity and low risk, their average annual return for the ten-year period was less than half that of the diversified portfolio—a high price to pay for greater stability. Moreover, money market returns provided the smallest margin over inflation in the same period.

Over the long run, owning a wide variety of investments is the best strategy for almost everyone, because most people hope their investments will meet a number of different goals. You may want to save for college expenses or your own retirement, to start a business, to supplement your pension, to set up an "emergency" fund—or pursue several goals at once.

HOW RISKY ARE THEY?

Low Risk
Money market funds
U.S. Treasury bill funds
Insured bond funds

Moderate Risk
Income funds
Balanced funds
Growth and income funds
Growth funds
Short-term bond funds
Intermediate bond funds
Insured municipal bond funds
Index funds
GNMA funds

High Risk
Aggressive growth funds
International funds
Sector funds
Precious metals funds
High-yield bonds (taxable and tax-free)
Commodity funds
Option funds

While no single type of investment can achieve all your goals, each one can make an important contribution to your long-term plan. Money market funds can provide a foundation of stability and liquidity that is ideal for the cash reserve you may need to tap on short notice. Bonds are good choices for steady, high income, while stocks (U.S. and foreign) have the greatest potential for superior, long-term returns and protection against inflation.

A diversified portfolio that includes the basic types of financial assets can provide attractive performance over time with moderate volatility. Of course, you must remember that diversification can reduce, but not eliminate, risk. As you begin to read more and more about investing you'll see this statement over and over: "Past performance cannot guarantee future results." Nevertheless, diversifying wisely can help you meet your important financial goals.

You Get Professional Management

It was apparent when we discussed the costs to you of owning a mutual fund that you pay for a fund manager's expertise. Behind each fund is a professional management team that controls the buying and selling of the securities in the fund's portfolio.

If you were to create your own portfolio of stocks and bonds, you'd have to monitor every purchase yourself. That can be a time-consuming and bewildering task. Research, tracking stocks, anticipating market trends, buying and selling. They might be fun for some, but the record keeping involved—especially with a moderate amount of turnover in your portfolio—isn't a trip to Disney World. In fact, you might even end up hiring trained professionals to manage the whole portfolio. With a mutual fund, you get that automatically, so all those tasks are performed for you.

You still have to keep track of the fund's performance (more on that later). But the key to the performance of any fund is the manager running it. Fund managers are responsible for all facets of a fund's portfolio—diversification of securities, buying and selling decisions, risk versus return, and investment performance. For all that responsibility, they pull down some weighty salaries. But unlike the compensation earned by some captains of industry, the earnings of these managers is tightly pegged to the performance of their funds. With most of their clients' levels of loyalty being only as deep as last quarter's return, superior performance is a must for a manager's continued survival.

Determining the Mix

While diversification helps reduce risk, the panoply of funds available to you allows you to find funds that meet your particular tolerance for risk. That might be based on your personality, your current financial situation, or your age. And it will probably change as you move through life.

Not only can you find funds suitable to your risk concerns, but you can mix and match funds with various risk levels in order to optimize your returns. Here are several ways that you might select a mix of stocks, bonds, money markets, and international securities to meet various risk levels.

The Basic Picture

If you're an aggressive investor, you can put 80 percent of your money in a stock fund and 20 percent into bonds. It's easy to be aggressive when you're a high roller or if you are young, because you have plenty of time to make sure your losses will be offset by your gains. "Young" is a relative term. It can include Generation X-ers in their twenties and Baby Boomers approaching 50. (If you are investing for your kids' or grandkids' futures, you might also invest aggressively.)

Moderate investors usually want to protect their principal, often because they're approaching retirement. But they don't want to give up on growth just yet. Usually between ages 50 and 59, these investors should put 60 percent of their money into stocks and 40 percent into bonds.

Conservative investors are determined to avoid risk. They might be especially cautious, but most often they are between the ages of 60 and 74, nearing retirement, and want to protect the purchasing power of their money. (And if they've been investing for years, they want to protect the nest egg they've built up.) They still need growth to offset inflation. A good mix for this kind of investment is 40 percent stocks, 40 percent bonds, and 20 percent money market funds. Senior citizens generally have the least risk tolerance. They're worried about outliving their money. They may even have to preserve their principal to live on it—no small chore. A good mix for this kind of investor is 20 percent in stocks (to help maintain the purchasing power of their money), 60 percent in bond funds, and 20 percent in money market funds.

Getting Specific

The beauty of mutual funds is that these broad mixes of stocks, bonds, and money market funds can be further refined.

An aggressive investor can divvy the stock portion of her portfolio among aggressive growth funds, small-cap stocks, or similar types of stocks in overseas companies.

Moderate investors can divide their stock portion between growth and income funds, international funds, and a bit in growth funds.

Conservative investors can choose for their portfolios from among U.S. and overseas growth and income funds, equity income funds, and short- or intermediate-term bond funds.

How Much Will It Cost You?

Don't be a ninny. Put aside all those pamphlets and take a minute to compare the expenses for the different mutual funds you are considering. Then choose the one that works best for you.

Fund Name	**Fund 1**	**Fund 2**	**Fund 3**
Load %			
Redemption Fee			
12b-1 Fee			
Switching Fee			
Maintenance Fee			
Expense Ratio			
Other Fees			
Minimum Balance			
Minimum Deposit			

Reduced Transaction Costs

Although there are costs related to investing in a mutual fund, those costs are nothing compared to the cost of trading individual stocks to build your portfolio. You pay a broker's commission on every stock you buy for your portfolio. And every time you sell a stock, you have to pay another commission. Commission costs—even with a discount brokerage—can be considerable.

With a mutual fund, you don't have to worry about any of that stuff. The fund performs such large transactions that the cost to each investor shrinks to insignificance.

What's also nice about being invested in a fund is that everything is done for you—right down to the end-of-year IRS tax forms and periodic transaction statements for your records.

RISK *is* not a *party* GAME

CHAPTER EIGHT

It's probably a compliment to the mutual fund industry that so many **neophyte** *investors may lose sight of some of the risks. The risks are real, though. And you should learn about them before you invest a* **penny.**

Certainly companies aren't above hyping their funds. But for an industry that deals with trillions of dollars, it has done a remarkable job of avoiding scandal and building a reputation that can be taken to the bank. Nevertheless, it's important for you to realize that a mutual fund is an investment, not a bank deposit—even if the fund is sold inside a bank. There's a warning that all funds declare but tend to bury in hoopla: Past performance is no guarantee of future returns. You should pay more attention to that warning than smokers pay to the caution on a pack of cigarettes.

You live with risk every day. Every time you sit behind the wheel of a car, you face risk. When you cross a street, you face risk. When you sun yourself in the summer, there's that pesky risk again. Unless you're an actuary at an insurance company, you probably ignore many of these risks because you face so many per day.

So don't be afraid to invest. However, it's important to understand the risks you take when you invest in various types of funds—for your own peace of mind and so you won't make mistakes once you're invested.

Risk Levels

In chapter three you took your pulse for risk tolerance, so you should have an idea at which funds to direct your attention.

For the squeamish, there are funds with low-level risks:

- Money market funds
- U.S. Treasury bill funds
- Insured bond funds

For investors with a little more grit, there are funds with a moderate level of risk:

- Income funds
- Balanced funds
- Growth and income funds
- Growth funds
- Short-term bond funds (taxable and tax-free)
- Intermediate bond funds (taxable and tax-free)
- Insured municipal bond funds
- Index funds
- GNMA funds

And for the real cowboys, there are high-risk funds:

- Aggressive growth funds
- International funds
- Sector funds
- Specialized funds
- Precious metals funds
- High-yield bond funds (taxable and tax-free)
- Commodity funds
- Option funds

Be Careful Out There

What specific risks will you face when you invest in a mutual fund? Let's take a good look at them before you make any decisions.

Market Timing

You never really know at what point in a market cycle you're investing. You may join as the market is climbing and have a rosy run, or you may invest at a peak and watch your initial investment slip in value. One way to mitigate the risk is through dollar cost averaging. We'll describe the ins and outs of this method later, but the idea is to invest a fixed amount of cash into your fund every month—even when the market is dipping. The result is, by the time you cash out of your fund the average cost of your investment will be far less than the market price of your shares.

Lost Opportunity

If you invest in a financial instrument that has a fixed return at a fixed rate, you expose yourself to a missed opportunity. If interest rates go up during that term, you won't be able to take advantage of them. For instance, if you bought a certificate of deposit for five years at 4.5 percent and interest rates rose to 5 percent during that period, you'd lose the opportunity to earn that 5 percent. You can cover yourself against that kind of risk, though, by staggering your maturities over five years. In the case of the CDs, one set would mature in year one, the next in year two, and so forth.

Credit Risk

When dealing with bonds, there's always the risk that a company won't be able to pay back the money. As we mentioned before, the lower a company's credit rating, the more likely it is to default on its debt. The simple way to avoid this risk altogether is to invest in U.S. Treasury bonds or the bonds of government agencies. Neither of those entities is about to go out of business any day soon.

Interest-Rate Risk

Interest rates are often mentioned in connection with bonds because bond prices and interest rates move in opposite directions. That's an obvious risk. What isn't as obvious is the effect that rising interest rates have on stocks. If interest rates begin to rise, it becomes more expensive for companies to borrow money. That can affect their bottom lines and in turn cause the share price of their stock to fall. It can also affect earnings and dividend payments because there's less money to distribute. All these developments can adversely affect the return of a mutual fund.

Diversification Risks

As we mentioned before, you want to make sure you don't have all your money invested in one kind of fund or bond. In good times, a focused investment like that might make you a bundle, but you run the risk of getting slammed in down times. You can hedge these risks in two ways: Own a mutual fund that invests in a broad spectrum of industries and diversify by owning both stock and bond funds.

Purchasing Power Risks

The dollar you earn today won't be worth a dollar tomorrow. Inflation insures that. So if you have an investment that gives you a fixed return, every year that investment loses purchasing power for you. For example, say you have a bond that returns to you $500 a year. The first year you own the bond, that $500 can buy a number of things. The next year, though, you can only buy some of those same items because inflation has increased their prices. The third year, you are able to buy even fewer items, and so forth.

The way to hedge against this erosion is to stay partially invested in stocks, which usually beat inflation by about 6.5 percent to 7 percent. In other words, inflation goes up, but your return goes up even faster. In periods of high inflation, you can further blunt this risk by investing in precious metals and energy funds—two sectors that do well during inflationary periods, because demand for these commodities remains constant.

Systematic Risks

Your mutual fund is a basket of stocks, bonds, or both. How the securities in the basket perform is tied to how all stocks and bonds do in their markets. If the markets go down, your return will go down, as will the price of your shares. That's a fact of investing. And it's called systematic risk. According to industry averages, 60 percent of the time a stock's price is going to move with the market.

Unsystematic Risks

About 20 percent of the time, a stock's price will shift due to information about the company, an

KINDS OF INVESTMENT COMPANIES

The *National Association of Stock Dealers Training Guide* classifies investment companies as follows:

- Diversified common stock funds
- Balanced funds
- Income funds
- Specialized companies funds (single industry, group of industries, or geographic region)
- Bond and preferred stock funds
- Money market funds
- Dual-purpose funds (companies that issue two classes of shares)
- Exchange-type companies funds (created to take advantage of tax loopholes that have been closed now)

industry, or the economy as a whole. That's called unsystematic risk. Diversification is a good way to blunt its barbs. If you have holdings across an industry, the performance of your portfolio will have a better chance of staying in the black when a few of your stocks react to bad news by dropping. As we've said before, that's what's so attractive about mutual funds.

Playing Turkey

When you make an investment, you stick out your neck—just as you do when you cross the street. If you look left and right and there isn't a vehicle in sight, the chances are good you won't be hit. But if you cross the street in traffic, your odds of becoming an asphalt pancake are greater. The question you have to ask yourself is, "How far out do I want to stick my neck?" Here are some numbers to consider when making your risk deliberations. In the past 60 years:

Stocks have grown an average of 10 percent a year. But in any given year, the price swing is an average of 21 percent. So you have a 66 percent chance (probability) of making a return between 11 and 31 percent.

U.S. government bonds grew at an annual rate of 4.3 percent during that period. The price swing for those securities was an average of 8.5 percent. So in a given year, you have a 66 percent chance of making between 4.2 and 12.8 percent.

Treasury bills grew at 3.4 percent, but with the price swing worked in, you have a 66 percent chance of earning between 0 and 6.8 percent in any one year.

Small-company stocks grew at 12.1 percent, but in any one year you have a 66 percent chance of earning between 23.8 and 38 percent.

Foreign stocks increased an average of 13.2 percent a year. But in any one year, you have a 66 percent chance of earning between 7.1 and 33.3 percent.

Foreign bonds grew at an annual rate of 8.7 percent. But in any one year, you have a 66 percent chance of earning between 2.6 and 18.8 percent.

Inflation grew at 3 percent. But 66 percent of the time it's somewhere between 1.8 and 7.8 percent in a given year.

Tools for Measuring Risk

One of the reasons you probably want a mutual fund is you want to do a minimum of financial legwork. Nevertheless, after checking mutual fund listings day in, day out, week after week, there may be a point when you feel you'd like to adopt a more sophisticated approach to ascertaining risk. For future reference, you might want to become familiar with these common measures.

- *Beta Coefficient.* This is the measure of a fund's risk relative to the entire market. A beta of one means the fund moves as the market moves. So if the market in general is returning 8 percent on your investment, your fund will give you a similar return. If the market moves down, your fund will go that way, too. The higher a beta, the greater the risk. So a fund with a beta of two means your gains will be twice the market's, but your losses will be twice as severe, too.

- *Alpha Coefficient.* Funds don't always perform the way their beta says they should perform. That's why we have an alpha coefficient. A fund's alpha tells you how it performed compared to how it was expected to perform (the beta coefficient). A positive alpha is good news for you. A fund with a 5.5 alpha means your fund manager earned 5.5 percent a year more than he should have earned given the beta of his investments.

- *Interest Rates and Inflation.* These two items are in the news almost every day. For good reason. They have an immediate impact on the outlook of investors. Let the market get a sniff of higher interest rates, and the sneeze can send stocks tumbling. And bonds, well, we've already noted what happens to bonds when interest rates go up: Bond prices go down. The rate of inflation, which influences the direction interest rates will go, also affects some stocks more than others. Automobiles are an example of one sensitive category; real estate is another.

Hang In There

As unnerving as risk is, there are rewards for investors who can stay their course through tempest and balmy times. The longer you hold your investment, the better the chances are that you're going to make money.

Also consider that by holding your investment for any ten-year period since 1926, you had a 4 percent chance of losing money. Compare that with a 30 percent chance of losing money in any year if you bought stock at the beginning of the year and sold it by the end of the same year during the last six decades after 1926.

Nevertheless, remember, there are no investments without risk. And take that warning seriously: Past performance is no guarantee of future return.

WHO *are* those fund *manager* TYPES?

CHAPTER NINE

Now you know a little about stocks and bonds. And something **about** *mutual funds. But you must be dying to know who has gotten their hands on your money. Who exactly are the players in this* **game?**

Before we get into the nuts and bolts of analyzing a fund—the prospectus—in chapter eleven, we should spend some time talking about the folks who you give your money to: the mutual fund companies.

A mutual fund company is a type of investment firm. The first investment firms began emerging in Europe at the beginning of the 1800s and spread to the United States by the latter part of that century, so they've been around much longer than mutual fund companies. As the nation entered the twentieth century, mutual funds began to pick up steam, but they were derailed—along with a lot of other business ventures—by the Great Depression.

What exacerbated this disaster for the investors in those early mutual funds was that the fund managers were allowed to use their clients' money to buy shares on margin. That means that instead of paying for the securities in a fund's portfolio at the standard dollar for dollar, they borrowed against the fund's assets to leverage the purchase of more stock. So, for example, if they had $100,000 in assets, they would use it to buy $400,000 in stock, effectively borrowing $300,000. That strategy worked as long as the market continued moving up, but once the crash occurred, everyone was left holding worthless IOUs.

This bit of history is important because you need to understand that once mutual funds found their feet again after the crash, Uncle Sam stepped in to make sure there were no encore performances of the mad leveraging that occurred in the '20s. The Investment Company Act was passed by Congress in 1940, which gave the federal Securities and Exchange Commission control over the industry. The new law required any fund wishing to sell shares to the public to be approved by the SEC first. Since the law was passed, it has been amended to further protect investors. Among those protections is the requirement that the industry must provide potential investors with information about its funds in a uniform format, called a prospectus (more about that in chapter eleven).

Today, investment companies, which are dominated by mutual fund companies, manage more than $3 trillion in investors' assets. That's a lot of money, to say the least. But it's less than half of the national debt and about 5 percent of the total financial assets in our economy. Simply, an investment company is an institution primarily engaged in the business of investing and trading securities. That sounds like a mutual fund. It sounds like many other kinds of companies, too. Brokerages, for example, and banks, and insurance companies. Even utilities invest and trade in stocks. But those companies aren't investment companies.

How Does a Mutual Fund Company Work?

Mutual fund companies fall into two distinct categories: open-end and closed-end. Sound familiar? It should. Open-end investment companies manage open-end mutual funds and closed-end investment companies manage closed-end funds. Technically, any investment company could be called a mutual fund, but the term is most commonly applied to open-end management companies. This use can be traced back to the 1940s, when promotional advertising appropriated the term for open-end funds.

The concepts that are used to describe an investment company are the same as those that define a mutual fund company: Investors who have common investment objectives give their money to a company to invest it for them. In return they're given shares in the mutual fund company.

The investors elect a board of directors for the mutual fund company. The board is responsible for making sure the fund sticks to its objectives. It also hires officers to run the company on a daily business. And it hires a management company to invest the cash flowing into the fund.

The management company makes the shares of the fund available to the public, and usually hires an investment manager and a team of advisers to oversee the fund's investments. The investment manager and his team of analysts use the best research available to study industry forecasts, economic conditions, the latest trading data, and which companies are likely to prosper under the prevailing conditions. The manager, as head of the team, is responsible for formulating the best strategy for meeting the fund's investment objectives. He is also the ultimate authority on what the fund buys and sells. He stands alone as the guy who must maximize his investors' returns and protect their principal from losses. When the final analysis is done, he gets the bouquets or the brickbats.

Funds also do business with a custodian, a transfer agent, and an underwriter:

- The custodian is usually a bank. It safeguards the fund's assets, makes the payments for the stocks the fund buys, and receives payments when the fund sells securities.

- The transfer agent performs record-keeping for the fund's shareholders. It issues new sales, cancels and redeems shares, and distributes dividends and capital gains to shareholders.

- The principal underwriter distributes shares to the public. An underwriter sells those shares directly to the public or to a broker-dealer, financial planner, insurance agent, or banker.

How Funds Sell to You

There are four ways a mutual fund can offer and distribute its shares to you:

1. Directly, without any intermediaries
2. Through an underwriter, such as a broker
3. Through a selling group
4. Through a company plan

Direct Sale

The simplest way for a fund to sell you its shares is directly, without a sales organization or any other middlemen. This is the classic distribution method for a no-load mutual fund. Load funds can also be sold this way, but, as we mentioned before, you'll still pay the load, but instead of a middleman getting it, the investment company will keep it.

Underwriter Approach

Mutual funds also sell their shares through underwriters, such as brokers. When brokers underwrite the sale of fund shares to the public, they buy the shares from mutual funds at net asset value. When brokers sell the shares to you, they collect a load for the sale. That load is the way brokers make their commissions. And it's why they want to sell the shares to you in the first place.

Brokers aren't allowed to speculate in mutual fund shares. They can't buy shares in anticipation of a sale. They can only buy shares in response to your order. That helps insulate the shares from speculative fluctuations.

Selling Group

Sometimes underwriters want to broaden their reach when selling shares. They do that by cutting in a selling group on the deal. The selling groups allow the underwriters to reach a broader audience. This creates another layer of hungry salespeople to feed.

The underwriter pays the selling group a selling concession for selling shares of a fund. Receipt of that concession is governed by a sales agreement that strictly regulates how a selling group may sell the shares. Ordinarily, the brokers only make money when they sell shares of a fund, but if you ask your broker to act as the middleman in a redemption transaction (when you cash out of a fund), you can also be charged a redemption commission. This fee would be in addition to any of the standard fees the fund may hit you with for cashing out. You could avoid it by redeeming your shares directly with the mutual fund company.

Plan Company

Yet another way to sell mutual fund shares is through a plan company. This is about as far away as you can get from the source of the shares. The plan company, like the selling group, sells shares to its members. The plan company accepts periodic payments from its members and with that money it buys mutual fund shares for its members. The greater the number of players who are involved, the less money there is from your initial investment that actually makes it into your personal account.

The Major Leagues

So who are these folks who are going to be handling your money? Here are some of the major players.

Charles Schwab

Schwab Funds is a family of no-load mutual funds that cover a wide spectrum of investing needs. The company has 24 equity, asset allocation, bond, and money market funds designed to provide low-cost, no-load investing. Schwab's funds have $38 billion in assets under management.

Dreyfus

Dreyfus is one of the nation's oldest and largest mutual fund companies. It also has a corporate symbol that weighs reassuringly in the minds of investors and noninvestors alike: the lion. In August 1994, Dreyfus merged with Mellon Bank Corporation, creating the largest combination of a banking firm and a mutual fund company in the history of the financial services industry. Dreyfus has more than 100 funds and $79 billion in assets under management.

Fidelity Investments

Fidelity was founded 50 years ago by Edward C. Johnson II on a simple premise: Work harder and smarter every day to help a small group of investors meet their goals. Today that "small group of investors" has grown to include corporations, not-for-profit organizations, financial institutions, and advisers, as well as millions of individuals worldwide. Over the years, Fidelity has evolved from a mutual fund company to a diversified financial services company, with such diverse offerings as benefits management, trust services, and global brokerage services. Fidelity is known throughout the industry as a technological leader. In 1996 alone, the company expected to invest some $500 million in hardware, software, and systems to analyze and research virtually every publicly traded company in the world and to provide its customers with the most up-to-the-minute information necessary to help them make sound financial decisions. Fidelity is America's largest privately held investment manager with more than $400 billion in assets under management.

Janus

For the past 26 years, Janus Funds has been managing mutual funds. Janus likes to think of itself as a different kind of mutual fund company. It shuns the Wall Street image for a more laid-back one befitting a firm based in Denver, located outside the Boston–New York mutual fund axis. According to top dog Tom Bailey, though, that doesn't mean the company isn't serious about investing. "For us, it's a passion," he says. "It's even more than that, it's a lifestyle." Janus has over $39 billion under management for 1.3 million investors.

Loomis Sayles

Loomis Sayles is one of the largest and oldest investment counseling firms in the United States. Established in Boston in 1926, the firm manages more than $45 billion in assets and employs 371 people. There are 184 professionals, 101 of whom are

Doing the Math

Not all prospectuses tell you what the annual return and yield of a fund was. But they all do give you the information you need to calculate it. Just plug the values from the prospectus into the following formulas.

The Annual Return Formula

[(YearEnd NAV + YearEnd Distributions – YearBeginning NAV) x 100]/YearBeginning NAV

Take the net asset value for the fund at the end of the calendar year you're performing the calculation for, add to it the distributions for the fund during that year, and subtract from it the net asset value of the fund at the beginning of the year. Multiply that number by 100 and divide that result by the net asset value of the fund at the beginning of the year.

For example, if a fund NAV started the year at $12.50 per share and ended it at $13.28 per share, and the year-end distribution amounted to $.32 per share, the annual return would equal 3.68 percent.

[($13.28 + .32 – $12.50) x 100]/$12.50 = 8.8%

The Fund Yield Formula

Total Distributions/YearBeginning NAV

Take the total distributions for the fund for the year and divide it by the net asset value for the fund at the beginning of the year. Using the same numbers, the formula would look like this:

.32/$12.50 = .03%

involved in portfolio management or research and have an average of 18 years of investment experience. In addition, almost three-fourths of the firm's investment professionals have qualified for the Chartered Financial Analyst designation, the Chartered Investment Counselor designation, or both—so they are trained professionals. Loomis Sayles has ten funds with $46 billion under management.

Scudder, Stevens & Clark

Scudder prides itself on innovation. It pioneered a "customer-first" philosophy in 1919, created America's first pure no-load fund in 1928, and developed the first international fund for U.S. investors in 1953. Scudder has 40 funds and $30 billion in assets.

T. Rowe Price

T. Rowe Price Associates is one of the nation's leading providers of no-load mutual funds for individual investors and for corporate retirement programs. The firm and its affiliates manage over $86 billion for 4.5 million individual and institutional accounts.

Twentieth Century-The Benham Group

Twentieth Century Mutual Funds and The Benham Group joined forces in 1995 to become the nation's fourth-largest family of no-load mutual funds. Recognized as a leading equity fund manager, Twentieth Century has provided investment management expertise since 1958. Benham, a respected name in fixed-income investing, started its first money market mutual fund for individual investors in 1972. Twentieth Century-Benham has 65 funds and $50 billion in assets under management.

Vanguard Group

The Vanguard Group, headquartered in Valley Forge, Pennsylvania, traces its roots to the founding of its first mutual fund, Wellington Fund, in 1928. Today, with net assets exceeding $200 billion, Vanguard ranks as one of the world's largest no-load fund complexes, serving five million shareholders in some 90 funds. With its broad array of no-load funds and an average expense ratio of just 0.31 percent, Vanguard is widely recognized as the mutual fund industry's lowest-cost provider.

WHAT *the fund* companies *do for* YOU

CHAPTER TEN

Granted, the most time-consuming part of **selecting** *a mutual fund is finding those that meet your investment objectives. It does require some research and a knowledge of the services they* **provide.**

No matter what you may hear from other folks, it is wise to do your own homework before you trust your money to even the most respected of firms. Take a look at a fund company's services, which vary from fund to fund. At the very least, the investment company that manages your fund should offer you some kind of accumulation plan, check writing privileges, the opportunity to move your money within fund families, a voluntary withdrawal plan, and an easy way to redeem your shares. Here's an explanation of each service, and some of the options you may come across. See which suit your fancy.

Accumulation Plans

As your investment increases within a fund, you'll want to maximize its growth potential by taking advantage of compounded growth. The more money you have in your fund, the greater the effect of any percentage of growth. Let's look at a very simple example: If you start with $5,000 in your fund and it returns an annual profit of 15 percent, you'll end up with $5,750. But if you have $5,050 in your fund, the same 15 percent growth would bring your account balance to about $5,758. That may seem like small potatoes, but think large. Over time, all those little figures (the extra $50, the extra $8) add up to increase your base amount painlessly. And eventually the "potatoes" added to the account will start to seem larger and larger.

But to do that, you need to accumulate shares in your fund through an accumulation plan. There are several types:

Automatic Reinvestment Plans

Almost every mutual fund offers an automatic reinvestment plan. (If yours doesn't, then maybe you should look elsewhere.) With this kind of plan, all the dividends and capital gains earned by your shares in the fund are used to buy more shares. And as the net asset value of the fund goes up, not only will the value of your original investment go up, but so will the value of the additional shares you've purchased through reinvestment.

When the dividends and capital gains earned by your shares in a fund are used to buy new shares in the fund, you usually don't incur any load charges. If a fund does charge a load for reinvesting distribution income, it will be spelled out in the fund prospectus. And if it does, you really should consider choosing another fund. (If you're investing in a no-load fund, you don't have to worry about charges for reinvesting distributions; there aren't any.)

After a dividend and capital gains distribution has been reinvested into your account, you will receive a notice from the company letting you know. It will spell out the amount of the distribution, the current NAV, the number of shares added to your account by the reinvestment, and the total number of shares in your account after the distribution.

Contractual Accumulation Plans

In addition to reinvesting your fund's earnings, you might also wish to invest some of your current income on a periodic basis. The title "contractual accumulation plans" sounds pretty formal, but it just means that you can arrange for the mutual fund company to make periodic withdrawals from your checking account and invest the money into your mutual fund. This not only accumulates shares in your account, but puts the dollar cost averaging strategy into play (more on that in chapter fourteen), which can help pump up your total return from the fund.

Voluntary Accumulation Plans

Suppose you feel the automatic withdrawal arrangement puts you in a bit of a straitjacket. Suppose you want to put more or less into your fund than your automatic amount? Maybe you want to skip a month. If you're a disciplined person, you can set up your own, voluntary, accumulation plan.

Then you can invest as much as you want, when you want, for as long as you want. However, to make the most of the technique, you still have to invest based on some time schedule—monthly, bimonthly, quarterly—and you have to invest a minimum amount—which isn't a problem since all funds have a minimum requirement for the purchase of additional shares, usually $100. But you can change your plan whenever you want without filling out forms or making calls to your bank. If you suddenly want to change your plan from $100 a month to $200 every six weeks, you can do it. The only person who will be the wiser is you.

Whether you choose a voluntary or automatic accumulation strategy, you will reap the benefits of compounding. When you make your initial investment, it compounds as it earns you dividends and capital gains. When you reinvest those dividends and capital gains, they, too, begin compounding by earning you even more dividends and capital gains. And if you choose a fund that invests in tax-free securities, you receive a third chance to compound, because the money that would otherwise have gone to pay taxes increases your base fund amount.

Retirement Plans

A retirement plan that makes use of mutual funds is similar to an automatic reinvestment plan. You arrange for money to be withdrawn automatically from your paycheck and deposited in the fund. It should be easy to find a mutual fund company that administers a tax-deferred retirement savings plan. In fact, you'd be hard pressed to find one that doesn't. These plans have become so commonplace that their cryptic names are readily recognized by the public:

- *IRA*. An Individual Retirement Account, which anyone can open up.
- *Keogh plan*. A retirement account for a self-employed person.
- *401(k) plan*. A retirement account that is opened by an employer for the employees.
- *403(b) plan*. A retirement account that is opened by a not-for-profit employer for the employees.

When you set up a retirement account, you can choose from most of the mutual funds that are out there. (If the retirement fund is established by your employer, you probably will have to choose from a select group.) So the principles of investing are the same. The added benefit is that you defer paying taxes on the account until you retire, when you will be taxed at a lower percentage.

However, if you make your mutual fund a retirement account, your investment company must reinvest your distributions back into the fund (instead of offering you the option of getting a check). And you can't withdraw any money before retirement, without paying serious penalties and taxes (although you may lend the money to yourself with certain restrictions). Still, it is an excellent way to invest for your retirement, especially if your employer chooses to make contributions to the fund on your behalf.

Check Writing

Many mutual funds and all money market funds let you write checks on your mutual fund account. There are two common restrictions imposed on this practice by the fund companies. They usually want you to maintain a minimum balance in your account, and the checks must be written for a minimum amount, usually anywhere from $100 to $500. You can always write checks for more than the minimum amount, as long as you maintain the minimum balance required in the account.

Fund Switching

Most investment companies let you transfer money among funds in their families. Often this can be done with a simple telephone call, although a very few companies accept transfers over the Internet, for now. Usually switching money among funds doesn't cost you anything, but some funds charge a fee for this service (so do many discount brokers). Check the fund's prospectus.

Why would you want to switch among funds? Remember our constant dollar strategy? When the balance in our aggressive fund exceeded our target balance, we had to move funds into our money market fund. That's a switch. And when the balance in our aggressive fund dropped below our target balance? We had to ship money into the account from the money market fund. That's another switch.

There are other, riskier strategies that involve fund switching. For example, market timing. If you see the market turning bearish, you could switch your money out of stock funds and into money market funds. Why? Because you would try to preserve your principal balance. If you left it in stock funds, a bear market would push stock prices down and erode your principal. Because money market funds have very little fluctuation, you would effectively freeze your principal. During a bull market, the reverse strategy would be in order. In either case, you need the ability to switch among funds. So you need the option to be offered by your mutual fund company.

Voluntary Withdrawal Plans

Just as you want your investment company to provide you with a service for automatically transferring money into your mutual fund, you probably want to be able to move money out automatically, too. In a voluntary withdrawal plan, you instruct your fund manager to make periodic withdrawals from your account and send the proceeds to your bank. The withdrawals can be calculated based on a fixed number of shares or a fixed dollar amount, which can usually be as low as $50. As with check-cashing privileges, you must be aware of any minimum withdrawal amounts and minimum balances. This service is very attractive to retirees who want a fixed amount of income periodically.

Redeeming Shares

All funds provide several ways to cash out of your account. You can use the mail—if you aren't in a hurry for your money. Or you can fax your redemption request to the fund company or redeem shares by phone. Currently, no funds let you redeem your shares over the Internet, but you can expect that option to arrive eventually.

THE *fund* prospectus *answers* IT ALL

CHAPTER ELEVEN

B*y federal law, every mutual fund must provide you with a* **prospectus** *before you buy any shares in the fund. This is a document that has lots of juicy financial* **details.**

The content of the prospectus is also regulated by law. That's to insure that the information is presented to you in a uniform and consistent manner. It enables you to compare one fund with another very easily. At first blush, that may not be apparent. Legal-looking documents have a way of making things look more obtuse than they actually are. But once you get the hang of looking at a prospectus, you'll buzz through them with a minimum of effort.

Some companies stick to the road map drawn by the Securities and Exchange Commission (SEC) and include in their prospectuses only the information they're required to include. These bare-bones prospectuses may be three or four pages in length. Other companies try to make the prospectus a sales tool. They include additional material to sell you on their fund. These prospectuses may be 15 or more pages long.

At a minimum, a prospectus must include a fund's financial history, investment objectives, and management data. Other requirements include:

The name and title of the portfolio manager. (Funds managed by a committee or index funds are excluded from this requirement.)

A discussion of the fund's performance—what happened during the previous year and why it happened.

A graph showing the fund's performance compared to relevant indexes over the previous ten years. The graph shows the performance of a $10,000 investment and must take into account all sales charges, expenses, and account fees.

A Tour of the Prospectus

The first page of the prospectus will show the date of publication, the name of the fund, the type of fund, and its major objectives.

Next, there's usually a table of contents. It will give you the lay of the land and cover most of the minimum topics. A typical prospectus can be divided into 17 key areas. Now that you know the key terms, some of the items will be self-explanatory:

1. *Name of the fund and the date of the prospectus.* The prospectus is updated every year to reflect changes in the fund, but changes can take place more often. In one prospectus, for example, all copies of the document circulated after April 1996 contained an amendment stating that the fund's custodian had changed.

2. *Required cover statement.* This tells you to read the prospectus before you invest in the fund. It also tells you where you can get additional information about the fund.

3. *Disclaimer.* This is required by the SEC. Basically it says you're a grown-up and you're responsible for your investments. It's up to you to accept or reject the decisions of the fund. In other words, if you don't like how the fund performs, it's up to you to get out. And if you lose money, you can't blame anyone but yourself.

4. *Statement of investment objectives.* Pay close attention to this one. You want the fund's objectives to jibe with yours. If they don't, look elsewhere. The statement usually describes the fund based on the information in chapter five, for example, "A growth and income fund that seeks a moderate return while reinvesting dividends."

5. *Fee table.* This lists any loads you may have to pay for entering the fund. It also lists the management fees, 12b-1 fees (marketing and distribution, or how the "free" prospectus is paid for), and other expenses.

6. *Per-share table.* This appears on the same page as the fee table. It gives you important information on the fund's performance. It shows you:

   - Expenses
   - Net investment income
   - Dividends from net investment income
   - Distributions from capital gains
   - Net increase in the fund's net asset value
   - NAV at the beginning of the year
   - NAV at the end of the year
   - Ratio of expenses to average net assets
   - Ratio of net investment income to average assets

- Portfolio turnover rate
- Number of shares outstanding

7. *Performance.* The prospectus may give you information about the yield and total return of the fund. Total return measures the gain or loss in the NAV of the fund after including reinvestment of its dividends and capital gains. This lets you compare one fund to another, or one fund to other kinds of investments.

8. *Investment policies.* These will show you how the fund decides what to buy and sell. There are almost as many reasons for choosing or selling a stock as there are mutual funds.

9. *Investment risks.* Here you'll find just how far the fund is willing to stick its neck out to make a buck for you. (Make sure it matches your own tolerance.) You'll also learn the restrictions the fund places on itself when making investment decisions.

10. *Portfolio turnover*. The holdings a fund had at the beginning of the year won't be the same as the holdings it has at the end of the year. This is where you can learn how much change there has been in the fund's portfolio.

11. *Information about the fund's investment adviser.* The name and address of the fund's investment adviser is listed here. You can also learn about the adviser's experience, services offered, and fees collected.

12. *Information about the transfer agent.* The transfer agent takes care of the bookkeeping for the fund.

13. *Shareholder rights.* This tells you that you are an equal partner in the fund and will receive the same return per dollar you invest as every other shareholder.

14. *Distribution.* You'll learn when your dividends and capital gains are declared and when they are paid.

15. *Taxes on earnings.* This section reminds you that you must pay taxes on the earnings of your fund—unless you're investing in a tax-free fund. It will also tell you when and how you can defer your taxes, such as if you are enrolled in a retirement fund.

16. *How to buy shares.* Who do you give your dough to? You'll find the answer to that question here. You can also learn about the minimum ante necessary to enter the fund and the minimum for subsequent investments. This section will also explain automatic investments, such as those made from your checking account each month.

17. *How to redeem shares.* This part of the prospectus tells you how to cash out of the fund.

Although the writing in prospectuses won't catapult them to the top of *The New York Times* best sellers list, you'll learn everything you need to know to make an informed decision about your fund. If you're not inclined to mull over all 17 areas of the prospectus, you should pay special attention to at least two of them: the investment summary and the summary of fees and expenses. The investment summary will tell you if your objective goals are compatible with the fund's objectives. The sum-mary of fees can be used to compare expenses among funds.

The prospectus is valuable to you because it prevents a fund from misrepresenting itself to you. And it protects the fund from lawsuits based on the failure to provide you with "full and honest disclosure."

Where Do I Get One?

There are a number of places where you can obtain a prospectus.

- *From a broker*. Keep in mind that brokers handle load funds so the prospectuses they have on hand are usually for those kinds of funds.

- *From the investment company.* You can write to the company or call their investor relations department. Most funds have an 800 number you can call to request information about the company.

- *From the Internet.* Many funds now allow you to download the prospectuses for their funds at their Web sites on the Internet. These prospectuses are usually in Adobe Acrobat format so you need an Acrobat viewer to look at them. This software can be downloaded for free from a number of locations on the Net. You can also request a hard copy of the prospectus at the Web sites of many funds.

Mutual fund companies are happy to send you a prospectus for any of their funds for free. In the package with the prospectus, you'll most likely find an application for the fund and the most recent financial report for the fund.

Other Documents You'll See

Just because you invest in a fund doesn't mean the goodies stop arriving in your mailbox. Every three months you'll receive a quarterly report. The fund manager or president of the fund will tell you how the fund performed during the period and how he expects it to perform in the future. You'll get the latest performance numbers for the fund in this report as well as historical numbers. And you'll get a list of the fund's holdings.

At the end of each year, you'll get an annual report that will wrap up how the fund performed for the previous 12 months.

Once you've looked over the prospectus for the fund and you're satisfied with what you see, the next step is to sign up. That's what we'll talk about next.

OPEN *and* contribute to *that* ACCOUNT

CHAPTER TWELVE

Y**ou've done your research and **studied** the prospectus. Now you're ready to open an account. First decide if you want a load fund or a no-load **fund.

If you decide to open an account with a load fund, a broker selling that fund will give you all the help you need to set up an account. And she should. She's taking a cut of your money for it.

If you're opening a no-load account, you'll have to put a little more effort into opening an account, but you'll save some money, too.

Step-by-step, here's what you would do to open a typical no-load fund:

1. Call the investment company.

2. Request a prospectus. If you're going to set up a retirement account with the fund, tell the sales representative that when asking for the prospectus. The application for a retirement account differs slightly from a standard account application.

3. Read the prospectus. Although you will be best informed if you read everything, make sure you pay close attention to the investment summary and the summary of fees and expenses.

4. From the prospectus, determine the minimum investment in the fund. If you're opening a retirement account, you can usually start with less than if you're opening a nonretirement account. You must invest the minimum amount, but you can invest more if you want to.

5. Send a check for at least the minimum amount and an application for each fund you select. Some companies let you invest in more than one fund on a single application as long as the accounts are registered in the same way and your check covers the minimum amount required by each fund.

6. On your application, you must note how you want the account registered (more on registering the funds in chapter thirteen). You also must indicate how you want your dividends and capital gains distributed. You can take them in cash or have them reinvested in the fund. If you reinvest them in the fund, you'll be able to take advantage of compounding interest, which means that you increase the amount of your principal investment. Any interest payments will be calculated as a percentage of that larger dollar investment—it often makes more sense than pocketing minuscle dividends!

   Take a look at the following table, which assumes a fixed interest rate of 8 percent:

Compounding Your Cash

Investment	Years Invested				
Per Month	5	10	15	20	25
$100	$ 7,348	$18,295	$34,604	$ 58,902	$ 95,103
300	22,043	54,884	54,884	103,811	282,308
500	36,738	91,473	91,473	294,510	475,513

7. Sign the application. After you send it in, you'll receive via mail a confirmation of your investment and your account number. The confirmation will include a deposit slip for your next deposit into the fund. Every time you make a deposit, you will receive a confirmation and a deposit slip.

A Word about IRAs

An Individual Retirement Account (IRA) is a mutual fund that has special tax benefits allowed by the Internal Revenue Service. But you've got to abide by certain rules to take advantage of those benefits. Those rules are set down in IRS Publication 590 and can be obtained free of charge by calling (800) 829-3676.

If you're going to use your mutual fund as an IRA, you should keep in mind that not all funds are suitable for this purpose. For example, why set up a relatively low-interest, municipal bond fund as an IRA when any fund you set up as an IRA (including those with high yields) will give you the same tax benefits?

Also, since you're establishing your IRA so you'll have something from which to draw when you retire, you don't want to make a high-risk fund your IRA. However, you may want to consider starting an IRA in an aggressive fund and rolling it over into a less aggressive fund type as you approach retirement.

Raising the Ante

Once you've opened your mutual fund account, you can either stay put and watch your money grow, or raise the ante by making additional contributions. It isn't required that you make additional deposits, but if you were smart enough to buy into a fund, you're probably smart enough to realize the benefits of disciplined, periodic investing.

One attractive aspect of investing in an existing account is that the minimum investment drops drastically. The exact minimum contributions are spelled out in your prospectus, but they can be as little as $25 (although the most common minimum investment is $100).

When you buy additional shares in your fund, you buy them at their net asset value at the time of the additional purchase. So you may have paid $10 a share when you entered the fund, but when you make your next purchase, the fund's NAV may be $12. Another time, the shares may be $14. You get the drift?

One relatively painless way to add to your investment is to reinvest all the dividends and capital gains the fund distributes to you. You can instruct the fund to do this automatically when you complete your fund application. Or you can amend your application later. Reinvested sums are not subject to the minimum requirements imposed on other share purchases. It is highly recommended that you reinvest your fund distributions so you can take advantage of compounding, which we illustrated earlier in this chapter.

Rely on Mr. Postman

It's easy to buy additional shares in your fund through the mail. When you applied for your fund, your confirmation from the investment company contained a deposit slip. Simply write out a check or money order, put it in an envelope with the deposit slip (the mutual fund company usually sends a postage-paid envelope, too), and mail it in.

Each time you make an investment by mail, or when the fund makes a distribution of income, you will receive a confirmation statement, also known as an Investment Account Statement. This statement will show:

- A trade date, which is the date you purchased your shares or a distribution was added to your account.
- The amount, in dollars, of the investment or distribution.
- The number of new shares the investment or distribution added to your account.

- The total number of shares you now own.
- The total value, in dollars, of your account.

Use the Wire

We live in an age of near-instantaneous gratification, so using the mail may not be fast enough for some investors. If that sounds like you, then consider using a wire transfer. The "wire" refers to the telegraph, although these transfers are now performed electronically over telephone lines (meaning you use the modem on your computer).

When you apply to your fund, you will be offered the option of purchasing shares via wire. You'll need to provide the name of your bank, its address, your account number, and a voided blank check. The fund will make the necessary arrangements for electronic transfers with your bank.

After you're set up to make wire transfers, you can call your bank during business hours and direct it to transfer money from your checking account to your fund. The bank makes an electronic transfer to your mutual fund account and the mutual fund company mails you a confirmation.

Transacting business electronically becomes crucial if you want to take advantage of a turn in the market. Ordinarily, those kinds of market turns are more important to someone speculating in stocks than someone who is investing in mutual funds, but if you need same-day turnaround on a transaction, the wire method will get it done for you. Before you choose this method for adding to your fund, you should check the fund application and query your bank about possible fees. You can get whipsawed if either the bank or the fund (or both) levy a fee.

Another kind of electronic transfer is called a "special purchase and redemption." You can set up this kind of transfer by special arrangement with your fund and bank. Like the wire transfer, this method provides a paperless way to transfer money from your bank account to your mutual fund. But this transaction can take up to two days to complete because, essentially, it is an electronic check that must be cleared through the Automated Clearing House (where all checks are validated). However, most banks and mutual funds won't charge you for a special purchase redemption because you're doing them a favor. The less paper they handle, the better they like it.

Set Up an Automatic Purchase

If you're so inclined, you can set up an automatic purchase arrangement for your fund. This works like an electronic wire-transfer purchase, except that it's automatic. When you apply to the fund, you instruct the fund company to make periodic, automatic withdrawals from your checking account—monthly, quarterly, whatever—and the withdrawal amount you specified is used to purchase shares. You buy the shares at the net asset value of the fund at the time the transfer is made. And you receive a confirmation by mail.

YOU'VE *got to* register *your* ASSET

CHAPTER THIRTEEN

W**hen you apply to a fund, you also have to **register** it with the investment company. That's a fancy way to define who owns the money and who has access to the **account.

Registering ownership is important now and for the future if you should die. Here are the different categories that you can select:

Individual Ownership

When you register your fund as an individual, you register it in your name only. That means you're the only person who can make deposits, move funds from the account into other funds in the family, redeem shares of the mutual fund, write checks on the account, request information, and close the account. You also must make provisions for disposing of the account's balance in the event of your death. Unlike life insurance, you can't name a beneficiary for your fund; you have to include its disposition in your will.

Joint Account

You also can register your account with another owner. If your account is registered in this way, you can sell or give away your share of the account—50 percent—but you can't leave it to anyone else when you die.

Here's a hypothetical example of how this form of registration works. Nick, a widower, checks the joint registration box on his mutual fund application and lists his daughter Noreen as the joint registrant. When Nick dies, Noreen will become the sole owner of the account—even if Nick says in his will that his entire estate should go to his other daughter Nina.

Tenancy in Common

When an account is registered this way, each owner has control over his or her share of the account. You can do anything you want to do with your share, including willing it to someone when you die.

In our example, if Nick wants to make sure Nina doesn't get excluded from his share of his mutual fund, he can register the fund as a tenancy in common with Noreen. When Nick dies, half the shares of the fund would go to Noreen and the other half to Nina, who is sole beneficiary of his estate.

Joint Account with Rights of Survivorship

Married couples can register their accounts with rights of survivorship. For legal buffs, this kind of account is known as "tenancy by the entirety." This kind of account fills in some of the blanks left empty when the owners of accounts registered in other ways (like trusts) die. In an account with rights of survivorship, the surviving spouse takes control of the fund when the other spouse passes on.

There are legal advantages to setting up an account this way. Those advantages have to do with probate. When you die, your estate must go through probate. Probate is the legal process for validating your will and executing the terms in it. The costs of probate—courts costs, legal fees, and other expenses—can be hefty. By registering your account as joint with rights of survivorship, the contents of the account can pass on to either survivor without the need of probate. However, remember that a tenancy-by-the-entirety agreement doesn't take the place of a will.

A Trust

Tenancy by the entirety is one way to avoid the legal vultures who circle your mutual fund when you die; another way is to register your fund as a trust. When you create a trust, a person called the trustee holds the title to the mutual fund account, which is the trust property for the benefit of a person known as the beneficiary. Trust accounts are usually created for estate purposes and to minimize the tax consequences on the estate of the trustee.

A common kind of trust is called a living revocable trust: "living" because you can manage it while you're alive and "revocable" because you can scrap it any time you want. By itself, this kind of trust won't save you taxes, but when used in combination with other estate planning techniques, it can blunt the bite the state will take out of your estate when you die. Living revocable trusts have three officers—the trustor, the trustee, and the beneficiary—and in most states, you can name yourself as all three. You also want to name a standby trustee and standby beneficiary who will fill in for you if you're unable to administer the trust. A bank or stock brokerage trust department is the best standby trustee because of their knowledge and expertise in trust management. Either a person, another trust, or an institution can be the standby beneficiary.

A gift trust is set up to benefit someone else and is commonly used to fund a child's college education. When setting up a gift trust, an investor establishes the account as a gift to an individual, who will receive gift trust shares on a specified maturity date. It is an irrevocable trust, meaning it cannot be changed or canceled. Neither the grantor nor the beneficiary can amend the terms of the trust in any way before the specified maturity date.

Because of the unalterable nature of the trust, only the person for whom accounts are established can benefit from this gift. The giver of the gift trust cannot receive monetary benefit.

You can open a gift trust for as little $500 and some funds allow you to make subsequent contributions as low as $50 by check, bank wire, or by automatic monthly investment.

Usually, the only person who can invest in a gift trust you set up is you. Your spouse or the beneficiary of the trust can't directly invest in the trust. (Although they could give the money to you and you could invest it in the trust for them.)

As trustee of the gift, you're the owner of record. No one else can exchange, redeem, or transfer the shares before the maturity date. The beneficiary may continue to own the trust after it matures, but additional investments cannot be made other than reinvestment of distributions, which is done automatically. Once the gift trust matures, however, no additional investments from any source can be accepted under the rules of the trust.

Setting up trusts can be a complicated business and it's advisable to consult an attorney before you wade too far into trust waters.

Registering a mutual fund sounds more complicated than it is. Once you understand these definitions, registration is usually as simple as checking a box on your mutual fund application. However, you may want to check with your accountant if you want to include the account as part of your estate planning.

How Much Should I Ante?

Once you've decided that you want to up the ante on your fund you still might have questions about how often the contributions should be made. Should you contribute periodically? Should you try to time your purchases? These are all questions you should be asking yourself, and we'll give you some answers in the next chapter.

YOU can be your own captain of FINANCES

CHAPTER FOURTEEN

It's** been said that **eternal vigilance** is the price we pay for freedom. It's also the price investors pay for financial success. There's a whole bag of tricks you can use to be sure those dollars keep flowing out of the **hat.

Once you've invested in one or more funds, you might want to kick back and let things take care of themselves. Don't. Use one of these strategies. There are several time-tested strategies you can employ to maximize your return on investment.

Buy and Hold

The simplest strategy is almost a nonstrategy: Buy a fund and hold it. After all, as we have mentioned before, the longer you hold a fund, the better your investment should perform. However, remember that the capricious nature of love is fine for films from the '40s, but it has no place in an investor's game plan. A common error made by inexperienced investors is to substitute *amore* for common sense. They fall in love with a mutual fund and coddle a loser long past the point where it nurtures—even if it becomes painful. There are plenty of winners out there. You found one once. You can find one again.

That's not to say that the buy-and-hold technique should be eschewed entirely. Just don't buy and hold and bury your head in the sand. Keep yourself abreast of your fund's performance, and observe the iron rule of vigilance.

Dollar Cost Averaging

A slightly more active approach is a strategy called dollar cost averaging. The idea behind this strategy is to get more bang for your investment buck. You must invest the same amount of money each time at regular intervals. When the net asset value of the fund is down you'll be able to buy more shares of the fund with this fixed amount than when the NAV is up. So, the end result is that you'll make more money than if you invested a larger lump sum in a fund at one particular point in time.

Dollar cost averaging is only slightly more effective than buy-and-hold (which is also known as lump-fund investing). The disadvantage here is that you only know when to buy shares in the fund, never when to sell them or to switch to another fund—two strategies that may help you generate larger profits from your investment. But it does take advantage of the ups and downs of the financial markets, enabling you to buy more shares of a fund when the market is down. And when the market rebounds, you profit from the shares you bought during the bear period.

In order for the strategy to work the best, you need to implement it during a bear market. But because bull markets generally last longer than bear markets, there may not be enough time to make this strategy competitive. During bull markets, a lump-sum strategy will blow the doors off the dollar cost averaging approach. However, you can offset this bull-bear dilemma by investing twice as much in your fund during down times as you do during up times.

You should also be mindful that it takes about five years for an investor to accumulate enough money with dollar cost averaging to create substantial profits. In the short-term, dollar cost averaging will lag behind other strategies.

Month	Investment Amount	NAV	Shares Purchased
January	$ 300	$30	10
April	300	15	20
July	300	20	15
October	300	30	10
TOTALS	$1,200	$22	55

This table shows you how dollar cost averaging works. It shows you the results of the strategy over ten months and assumes you will invest a fixed amount of $300 each quarter. During this period the net asset value for the fund fluctuated between $15 and $30.

In January, when the NAV was at $30, your $300 bought ten shares. In April, you bought 20 shares at $15; in July, 15 shares at $20; and in October, ten shares at $30. Over the entire period, you would have invested $1,200 into the fund and purchased 55 shares (now worth $1,650). If you had invested that $1,200 in a lump sum into the fund in January, you would have had only 40 shares worth $1,200 by October.

But don't you lose earnings by failing to leave your $1,200 in the fund for an entire year? The answer is yes, but you make it back in other ways.

Let's say your fund had a yield of 8 percent for the year. If you had invested a lump sum of $1,200 in January, you would have earned $96 at the end of the year. By using dollar cost averaging instead, your earnings picture looks like this:

Month	Amount Deposited	Months in Fund	Dividends Earned
January	$300	12	$24
April	300	9	18
July	300	6	12
October	300	3	8
TOTAL DIVIDENDS			$62

You can see that your earnings take a hit. With the lump-sum investment, you would have earned $96; with dollar cost averaging you only earn $62 (and wish you had the additional $34). But you have to remember that you now hold more shares. With the lump-sum approach, your shares at the end of the year would only have been worth

$1,200, but now you have shares worth $1,650. With the lump-sum method, your investment would only be worth $1,296 ($1,200 plus $96), but because you used the dollar cost averaging method, it is worth $1,712 ($1,650 plus $62). That's $416 more!

It should also be noted that you would retain more of your earnings with dollar cost averaging since you would pay income tax on only $62 instead of $96.

It's easy to implement a dollar cost averaging strategy for most funds. You can do that by choosing to make automatic deposits into your fund when you apply for it.

Which funds are good candidates for using the dollar cost averaging method? Volatile funds. You want one with yo-yo activity so you can take advantage of drops in the fund's price. With this strategy, the higher the beta of the fund (the measure of its volatility), the better. Look for funds with betas over one. But you also want a fund that's a solid long-term performer and has consistently outperformed its peers. It should also have some resiliency, so take a look at how well it bounced back after bad years such as 1973, 1979, 1981, 1987, 1990, and 1994.

Fine-Tuning with Value Averaging

An investment strategy called value averaging fine-tunes the dollar cost approach. This fine-tuning can improve the potential of your averaging strategy, but it requires a little more diligence on your part.

In the following table, you can see how value averaging works. We assume you want your investment to increase by $1,000 a month.

Month	Start Value	End Value	Reaction
January	$10,000	$11,000	Do Nothing
February	11,000	10,000	Invest $2,000
March	12,000	13,500	Sell $500

You start in January with $10,000. At the end of the month, the investment in your fund is worth $11,000. Since your goal is to increase the value of your investment by

$1,000 a month, you've met your goal, and you don't have to do anything in January.

You begin February with $11,000. At the end of the month, the value of your fund has dropped to $10,000. To make your goal, you've got to invest $2,000 into your fund. This takes advantage of the drop in the fund's share price that month.

March starts with your account balance at $12,000. A surge in the share price of your fund brings the month-end balance to $13,500. This exceeds the goal you've set for the fund so you should sell $500 in shares, and reinvest the money elsewhere.

If you look at this system closely, you'll see what you're doing is buying low and selling high. Even a professional fund manager can't ask for a better strategy than that.

Studies have shown that during the past six decades, value averaging has outperformed dollar cost averaging as an investment strategy. During the period from 1926 to 1989, if you adjusted your portfolio four times a year using value averaging, your average annual growth rate would have been 12.76 percent compared to 11.42 percent with dollar cost averaging. If you adjusted your portfolio once a year, the rate is slightly lower: 12.54 percent for value averaging versus 11.41 percent for dollar cost averaging.

Average Combinations

There's no law that says you have to use one form of averaging to the exclusion of the other. You can mix strategies and fund objectives to further enhance your returns.

For example, you can use dollar cost averaging with an income fund and value averaging with an aggressive growth fund. You would deposit a fixed amount at regular intervals in the income fund account to take advantage of dollar cost averaging. In the aggressive growth fund, you would set your growth goal for value averaging. Then, if you meet your goal for the month, you stand pat; if your fund underperforms, you transfer money from the income fund account into the aggressive growth fund to meet your goal; if the aggressive growth fund exceeds your goal, then you transfer the excess to the income fund account.

The easiest way to implement this strategy is to move the money around within a family of funds because you can usually initiate the transaction with a simple phone call.

A variation of the combination approach is called constant-dollar investing. First, you set a ceiling for your aggressive fund—say $5,000. Then, once a year, you move money between that fund and a conservative fund, such as a money market or bond fund, depending on the aggressive fund's performance. If the amount in the aggressive fund exceeds $5,000, you move the excess into the conservative fund. If the amount in the aggressive fund is below $5,000, you return the balance to the ceiling amount by moving money from the conservative fund. The net result of this strategy is the same as the others we've discussed. You buy shares at low prices and sell them at higher prices.

And the variations keep coming. Instead of making your constant a dollar amount, you can make it a ratio. For example, you start with $10,000. You put $5,000 in a stock fund and $5,000 in a bond fund. The ratio is one-to-one. Once a year, you would check the accounts and adjust them so they reflect the ratio. So if at the end of the year, your stock fund had $5,400 and your bond fund had $5,100, you would move $150 from the stock fund to the bond fund so you would have $5,250 in each.

Value Ratio Investing

This method of flipping between funds is the basis of another strategy called value ratio investing. The hinge for this strategy is the price-to-dividend ratio of the S & P 500, which will give you an idea of whether the market is overvalued or undervalued. If it's overvalued, you allocate more of your investment to the conservative fund. If the market is undervalued, then you allocate more of your money to the aggressive fund.

As a rule of thumb, the market is overvalued when the price-to-dividend index is 30 to 34. That means, on average, an investor must invest $30 to $34 to get $1 in dividends. When the index is at 20 or less, the market is undervalued.

Check out some of the different scenarios shown in the following table:

Value Ratio Investing for Stock Portfolio

Price-to-Dividend Index	How to Allocate Investment	
34	100.0%	in conservative funds
30 to 33	87.5%	in conservative funds
	12.5%	in aggressive funds
23 to 29	62.5%	in conservative funds
	37.5%	in aggressive funds
20 to 22	37.5%	in conservative funds
	62.5%	in aggressive funds
Less than 20	100.0%	in aggressive funds

This table assumes you have all your money in stock funds. If you'd like to divide your portfolio between money market and stock funds, the next table has some suggestions for appropriating your money with that approach in mind.

Value Ratio Investing for Stock and Cash Portfolio

Price-to-Dividend Index	How to Allocate Investment	
34	50.0%	in money market funds
	50.0%	in conservative funds
32 to 33	15.0%	in money market funds
	75.0%	in conservative funds
	10.0%	in aggressive funds
30 to 31	10.0%	in money market funds
	55.0%	in conservative funds
	35.0%	in aggressive funds
23 to 29	50.0%	in conservative funds
	50.0%	in aggressive funds
20 to 22	37.5%	in conservative funds
	62.5%	in aggressive funds
Less than 20	100.0%	in aggressive funds

This approach, which is more complicated than dollar or value averaging, can outperform both those strategies. Studies have shown that moving among conservative and aggressive stock funds resulted in annual gains of 14.2 percent over ten years and 13.7 percent over five years. For cash and stock portfolios, the performance was even better: 15.5 percent over ten years and 16.8 percent over five years.

These strategies of moving money among accounts works especially well in IRAs and other retirement accounts because you won't have to pay taxes on the gains. If your funds are taxable, you can pay from 15 percent to 39.6 percent of your profits to the U.S. Treasury come income tax time.

Market Timing

The strategies we've discussed so far are disciplined and systematic methods for improving the return from your mutual fund. There are less disciplined and systematic methods, too, like market timing. All that means is that you try to make an educated guess about what the market is going to do next. The systematic strategies take advantage of turns in the market but, really, they serve as a series of checks and balances. Market timing can turn out to be no more than a stab in the dark, and it isn't recommended for novices.

In fact, it probably should be prohibited for many professionals. Over the past 20 years, the S & P 500 has grown at an average of 12.8 percent per year. Over those 240 months, if a market timer failed to guess the five best investment months during that period, his return would have dropped to 9.3 percent.

So far, you've learned three good rules to remember: Stay invested, stay alert, and stay away from trying to time the market.

HEY *captain,* stay vigilant *about the* MARKET

CHAPTER FIFTEEN

E**very day, newspapers devote a page or more to fund activity. Everywhere you look, newsstands **bulge** with magazines committed to dissecting financial trends. Use these resources to stay on top of **things.

Newsletters that promise proprietary savvy proliferate like mushrooms after a rain. And the volume of financial and fund information on the Internet will muddle your mind faster than a fifth of tequila. The exploding popularity of mutual funds has captured the attention of the folks who like to bring you information. And that has made the task of keeping tabs on your mutual fund investment easier than ever before. There's no excuse for not staying informed.

Read All about It

The daily newspaper remains a staple of investment information, although the business coverage can be pretty skimpy outside major media markets. Nevertheless, almost without exception, even the smallest daily fills up one or two pages with business "agate"—the stuff printed in a type the size of which only an eagle could love. But look sharp: Embedded in this fog of print are the numbers you need to monitor your mutual fund's performance. You should refer to these pages as religiously as some folks check the baseball box scores.

Once you have a fund to follow, you'll appreciate the information so much that you'll wonder why the newspapers don't devote more space to this important topic. Why don't they add a few more columns of information on each fund? Why not goose up the type?

Better yet, you'll soon be able to decipher the numbers that seem to be swimming across the page. First, you'll notice that the information is grouped alphabetically by mutual fund investment company. The company names are usually spelled out pretty much in their entirety, so they're easy to identify.

Under each firm name is an alphabetical list of fund families. And if the company is a giant, like Fidelity Investments, the list might be long. It's a little more difficult to identify an individual fund family because many of the names are abbreviated to conserve space. They may even be barely recognizable. But take heart, you'll quickly learn to recognize those funds that are holding your money!

The columns that appear beside each fund name vary from newspaper to newspaper. But every paper will give you the previous day's net asset value and the change in price of the fund's NAV—prices change all day so the number you see will be for the close of business. In addition to those numbers, some papers will publish a fund's load. Others will print the fund's expense ratio. Still others may list the fund's return over a certain period of time. What the number represents, though, will be clearly identified at the top of the column where it appears. Although most funds are displayed regularly, from time to time your fund listing may be cut due to lack of space.

Also sprinkled throughout the newspapers' mutual fund tables are letters that refer you to footnotes for additional information. Here are some of the most popular:

e is an abbreviation for ex-distribution. That means the fund distributes a dividend or capital gains (or both).

x stands for ex-dividend. From the time the fund declares dividends to the time it pays them, the fund is said to be in ex-dividend. During this period, anyone who buys shares in the fund will not be able to collect dividends until the next period. That's because it takes time for a fund to calculate how dividends should be distributed.

nl or **n** means the fund is a no-load fund.

p means the fund charges a 12b-1 fee (for marketing and distribution).

r stands for redemption charge.

t means the fund charges both a 12b-1 fee and a redemption fee.

Usually, you can get the most in-depth information from the Saturday or Sunday papers, which frequently print the weekly performance of mutual funds. These tables vary from newspaper to newspaper, too, but they usually include the high and low net asset value for each fund for the week, as well as the week's change in NAV.

Professionals and investing enthusiasts turn to publications like *The Wall Street Journal* and *Investor's Business Daily* because they offer the best coverage of financial information. And *Barron's* is an excellent magazine for weekly analysis of financial developments. But the average investor will find that the local dailies provide most of the basic information.

Another source of timely financial information are weekly business journals. Many major media markets have these feisty publications, which concentrate on local players in the financial markets. A chain of these weeklies is operated by American Cities Business Journals located in Charlotte, North Carolina.

The Glossy Approach

Although magazines can't provide you with the timely information newspapers can, they can give you more in-depth data on funds and financial markets. They also tend to give you a longer-term look at a fund's performance. Periodically magazines rank funds by performance and objective as well as classifying funds by type, risk rating, minimum investment, load, total return over one, five, and ten years, and price range over a 52-week period. Information on fund managers and how to contact a fund are also part of these editorial packages. Many of these magazines can be found on the newsstand. Try *Kiplinger's Personal Finance Magazine, Mutual Fund Magazine, Money, Worth,* and *Forbes.*

Handmade Productions

In addition to magazines, a whole industry has emerged around creating newsletters for mutual fund investors. But be forewarned: Newsletter subscriptions tend to be expensive—and everyone has an agenda. It would be foolish to make decisions about your money based on the advice of any single source. Read as much as you can and draw your own conclusions.

No-Load Fund Analyst. This newsletter focuses on a small universe of the better-known no-load funds. It contains economic analysis as well as in-depth analyses of events in the mutual fund industry. Closed-end funds are also covered. Unlike most newsletters, this one contains personality profiles of fund managers and keeps tabs on them as they move from company to company (many investors like to stick with the same person whose decisions have made money for them in the past). Two refreshing features of this publication are that it doesn't promise to make its readers millionaires, and its editors don't use it to tout their investment management business.

Mutual Fund Monthly. This newsletter is built around interviews with different portfolio managers. You can use it to learn what the managers of some leading funds think about the outlook for the stock and bond markets.

No-Load Fund Investor. Read it to get advice about which no-loads are best for short-term investments and which are better for the long term. You can also learn how to put together a portfolio.

The Money Experts Newsletter. Spawned by a local talk-radio program in Boston, this newsletter focuses on financial advice for the individual investor. It is better looking than many of its ilk, and the publication always includes an article or two about mutual funds. A recent sampling: "Advice About Closed-End Mutual Funds: For Most—Don't Buy 'Em!"; "Aggressive Growth Funds Grow Slowly in 1996"; and "Using Index Funds to Improve Your Chances of Beating the Average Fund."

Donoghue's Moneyletter. When recommendations are made for funds in this newsletter, current performance is given the most weight. The publication looks at short-, intermediate-, and longer-term performance to create ratings for funds, but "what did you do for me today?" plays the most important role in these calculations. The newsletter has a simple philosophy: Stay invested in the best performing funds.

Jay Schabacker's Mutual Fund Investing. This newsletter uses a combination of stock and bond indicators to identify top-performing funds. Once those funds are identified, the publication makes recommendations for buying and selling them. If you follow the advice, be prepared to give your touch-tone finger a workout.

The Mutual Fund Letter. Long-term performance is the only meaningful criterion by which to judge a fund, according to this newsletter. The editor of this publication looks at a fund's holdings to see if they match its objectives. When it finds a good fund, it recommends investors hold it for the long term.

United Mutual Fund Investor. Also wedded to a long-term approach to investing, this newsletter looks at a fund's performance compared to its peers and the market over the long haul. It likes funds with good performance in two categories: one year and three to five years.

Mutual Fund Forecaster. If you believe in the power of quants—those Wall Street wizards who use higher math to make their masters millions—you'll like the approach of this newsletter. It uses mathematical research to analyze the past and make one-year profit projections for more than 1,000 stock funds.

Income & Safety. This does for bond funds what the *Mutual Fund Forecaster* does for stock funds.

Stockmarket Cycles. A newsletter for the switching set, this publication monitors market trends and cycles and advises its subscribers when to switch between stock and money market funds.

InvesTech Mutual Fund Adviser. This publication gives advice about how to structure your portfolios based on an analysis of economic and fund performance trends.

Growth Fund Guide. Market timing is the aim of this publication. It surveys the financial markets and offers tips to its subscribers about when to move money into conservative or aggressive mutual funds.

Free Resources

Newspapers! Newsletters! Magazine subscriptions! You might begin to think that mutual fund research is almost a hidden "load" you have to pay to become an investor. It doesn't have to be. There are tools for those who believe that the best way to make money is to save it.

One inexpensive way to garner fund information is to go to the public library. Not only will you find many of the newspapers and magazines listed above, but you'll also probably find these invaluable reference works:

Morningstar Mutual Funds. Every other week, Morningstar publishes reports on more than 1,200 stock and bond funds. Each one-page report is packed with information about a specific fund. The funds are rated by the company using a star system; funds with four or five stars will give you the highest return for your money with the least amount of risk. The report also evaluates each fund, lists its 25 largest holdings, and compares its performance in down markets to similar funds.

The Value Line Mutual Fund Survey. More than 2,000 funds are scrutinized by this publication based on the fund's investment objectives. Funds are rated by number. One is the best; five the worst. The report also describes the fund's holdings, meaning the companies that make up its portfolio, and gives information about its performance in up and down markets.

Standard & Poor's/Lipper Mutual Fund Profiles. This publication contains half-page reports on about 1,000 mutual funds. The reports describe how a fund's performance stacks up against other funds in bear and bull markets and lists the fund's five largest holdings with their year-by-year returns.

The CDA/Wiesenberger Mutual Funds Panorama. For the long-term investor, this annual volume is a treasure chest of information. It is jam-packed with facts about the ten-year performance of more than 3,400 funds and offers a nice introduction to mutual fund investing.

The Horse's Mouth

While it's fine to seek published advice about funds you might like to buy, don't be shy about contacting the fund companies for information. All the funds have investor relations departments and you'll find them staffed by some of the most helpful people in any business. With a simple phone call—in many cases, toll free—you can find out the current NAV, yield, price change, dividend, or almost any other information about the company or its funds.

In addition, these companies are required by law to publish periodic reports about their funds. You can call the company and ask for the latest quarterly, semiannual, or annual report of any of its funds. The reports contain some marketing fluff, but there are real nuggets in them, too. They list the fund's holdings, for example, and disclose the fund's performance record for the period covered by the report. In fact, these free reports can provide much of the information someone else would charge you for.

The Net

As timely as newspapers are, as deep as magazines delve, as voluminous as reference books have become, there is one medium that rolls all those qualities into one package: the Internet. For investors armed with a computer and a modem, the Net is a paradise of information. What's out there in cyberspace and how to find it is the subject of our next chapter.

SURF *the* information *playground* ONLINE

CHAPTER SIXTEEN

*For the mutual fund investor, the Internet can be a **gold mine** of information. And best of all, it's accessible from your desktop. With a click of your mouse, you're in touch with a wealth of financial **resources.***

Need some news about a company? Go to an online news service or search the Internet for related articles. Need a NAV? Log onto a company Web site and get it. Need to chat with fellow investors about aspects of investment strategy? Subscribe to an online newsgroup.

In this chapter, we'll tell you how to get connected, then direct you to some of the best Internet sites for gathering information. We just summarize the features of the site, so we'll assume you have become familiar with the investing terms used in this book. If you feel a little confused, that's okay. A quick look in the glossary at the end of the book should refresh your memory.

Getting Connected

In recent years, cyberspace has been divided into two camps between online services—America Online, Prodigy, CompuServe and the Microsoft Network—and the Internet service providers.

All the online services offer access to the Internet and an e-mail account. These services are popular because they're relatively easy to set up and use, they give you free software to access their systems, and setting up is as easy as installing an application on a computer. They also give you content—sites and information you can obtain only as a member of the service.

Internet service providers (ISPs) will give you access to the Internet, an e-mail account, and some file space so you can set up your own Web page, if you want to. They usually don't have their own content, but a few do, such as GNN (which is owned by America Online). In many cases, you have to obtain the software to use an ISP on your own initiative (although outfits like Spry will provide the software for you). Once you obtain the software, you have to set it up for your particular ISP. This requires familiarizing yourself with Internet mumbo jumbo like domain names and POP server addresses. It isn't rocket science, but it takes some cerebral cooking. However, larger ISPs like AT&T will provide you with a package that makes it easy to become a subscriber.

Whether you opt for an online service or an ISP, make sure it offers a local access number. Some services supply 800 numbers you can call to access their computers, but then you are charged by the minute for access time. You should probably forget about those services because the toll charges you'll accumulate can break your financial back.

The death of online services has been predicted for many months now, but they still survive and continue to add members. America Online remains the strongest player. CompuServe has announced that it is withdrawing from the consumer market. Prodigy limps along, but has started a new service, Prodigy Internet, which shows some promise. Prodigy Internet is sort of a modified ISP. It will provide you with everything you need to access the Internet, so it's as easy to set up as an online service, and it uses a standard Web browser—the software you need to view information on the Web.

It also has the advantage of having a proprietary access system with broad geographical penetration so the chances are good it'll have a local access number near you. The Microsoft Network (MSN) was launched as a typical online service, but has been revamped as a hybrid ISP/online animal.

America Online

AOL has some of the best content of all the online providers. In addition to sections operated by several of the major fund companies, AOL's Mutual Fund Resource Center has a nice package of services for the investor. These include:

- Morningstar (an abbreviated version of the reference book version)
- Business Week Online Mutual Fund Center
- Consumer Reports on Mutual Funds
- Decision Point Mutual Fund Center (a treasure chest for wannabe quants)
- Market News
- Nightly Business Report (the online version of the PBS TV show)
- Real Life's Mutual Fund Mania
- Worth Online Fund Focus (a service put together by *Worth* magazine)
- FundWorks (a feature loaded with fund-specific information)

Prodigy

Although the major funds don't have much of a presence here, Prodigy is a good source of business news. The service is in the process of moving much of its content to the Web and is in the forefront of developing what may be a model for the online service of the future.

News You Can Use

There's plenty of financial news on the Net, some good, some bad, some bizarre. The great thing about the Internet is that anyone can become a publisher. It's the worst thing about the Internet, too, because you must constantly judge the worth of the information you collect. That's why it makes sense to stick to established sources if you're looking for financial news.

Wall Street Journal Interactive

When it comes to established news sources, you can't do better than the Wall Street Journal (wsj.com). This interactive edition is updated throughout the day and it is a lot more colorful visually than its printed brother. The Journal also contains features that are not found in the print edition, such as livestock quotes and the ability to create a personal portfolio that's updated automatically. If you subscribe to the print edition, the online version will cost you another $29 a year; otherwise, an annual subscription costs $49.

USA Today Money News

While the print version of *USA Today* has been referred to as McPaper, the online version (www.usatoday.com/money) has much more substance. The flashy graphics are still there, but there's a depth of information that is missing from the print edition. The Money section includes a mutual fund subsection that contains information on fund performance and links to news stories about the financial industry. The one drawback to the site is it isn't updated as often as some of the other news sites. But it's free!

NY Times on the Web

The online version of the nation's paper of record (www.nytimes.com) doesn't differ much from its print edition, but if you don't buy the *Times* every day, that shouldn't bother you. You can find stock quotes here, too, as well as the personal portfolio feature. It is also free, although you must be a registered user.

CNN Financial Network

The financial news keeps flowing into this site continuously (www.cnnfn.com). In addition to quotes and financial data, the site posts the latest rumors through its Grapevine feature and includes links to other business resources on the Web.

Searching for Other Articles

If, for some reason, you can't find what you need in any of the major publications, you can always search the entire Internet. To do that, you use one of the search engines (or "bots," those software agents that trawl the Internet for information), which will return a list of articles or Web sites that may contain what you want.

Certainly searching on the Web still has a long way to go. Many times a searcher will get hundreds of "hits" that are totally worthless. Although some search engines let you narrow your searches by using Boolean logic—a fancy name for using "and," "or," and "not"—many don't. Nevertheless, search engines provide an essential service. If you already know how to use search engines, you can skip to the next section. These are the major search engines:

Yahoo!

An apocryphal rumor made the rounds recently. It said that Netscape and Yahoo! were merging. The name of the new company? Netanyahu. A silly joke, perhaps, but it illustrates how visible one of

DUKE OF URL

To find a page on the Web, you have to access its site address, called a URL (uniform resource locator). It may look something like this: http://www.yahoo.com. The "http://" is standard to all URLs—some references will drop it when they refer to a Web site. The "www" in the URL stands for World Wide Web—the most **popular** part of the Internet. In fact, when many commentators talk about the Internet, they're really just talking about the Web.The next part of the URL is the pathname. It describes the location of the Web page on the computer, also called a **server,** where the page resides. The final part of the URL identifies the type of organization that is running the server: ".com" means a commercial enterprise; ".edu" is an educational enterprise; and ".net" is a network, such as an Internet service provider. Although this may sound **esoteric** to you, it will come in handy when you must memorize a URL.

the Web's most popular search engines has become. Comics can even make jokes with it and a mainstream audience will "get it."

Yahoo! (www.yahoo.com) is organized around categories. It starts with broad categories that are linked to continually more defined subcategories. You can "drill" down through the categories by clicking on its links (text underlined and in blue) or you can enter a search term and find the links at the site that contain that term.

Yahoo! catalogs Web sites so you'll only get a "hit"—an Internet search result—if your search term appears in the title of the Web site. However, if Yahoo! can't find your search term at its site, it will search the Alta Vista engine for you. Yahoo! receives about a million hits a day from Internet searchers.

Alta Vista

Digital Equipment created Alta Vista (www.altavista.com) to demonstrate the speed of its alpha processor. It proved its point. Alta Vista is one of the fastest search engines on the Web. It indexes about 50 million pages, including Usenet newsgroups, which are freewheeling discussion groups that sometimes border on anarchy. Alta Vista lets you perform relatively sophisticated searches of its material. You can do Boolean searches and use proximity criteria, or tell the Alta Vista to find a search term within so many words of another key word. This helps weed out a lot of worthless hits. Alta Vista receives about 16 million hits a day from Web searchers.

HotBot

HotWired, the online affiliate of *Wired* magazine, by Inkomi, a software company, operates a search engine called HotBot (www.hotbot.com). HotBot's approach to surveying the Web is a little different from other Web ferrets. It uses a distributed network of computers to perform its searches. This enhances the performance of the engine and provides searchers with more relevant results. HotBot is also very conscientious about cataloging Web pages soon after they appear on the Internet—sometimes within days.

Hardware Requirements

To take advantage of all the resources that are available in cyberspace to investors, you need to make sure that your computer has a few basic things:

- **A Modem.** The faster, the better. The fastest modem for residential telephone lines operates at 33.6 bps, but 56 bps modems are expected to be entering the market in 1997. You can get by with a 28.8 bps modem, but anything slower will be sheer torture if you have to stay online for any length of time.

- **An Internet Service Provider.** This is the company that connects you to the Internet. Some companies provide you with basic Internet access and e-mail. Others, like America Online, provide you with much more. Most novice cybernauts start with a service like America Online because it's easy to use, then move on to an ISP.

- **A Web Browser.** This is the software that lets you view information on the World Wide Web, which is part of the Internet. The major Web browsers are Netscape Navigator and Microsoft Internet Explorer.

ELECTRONS AS MONEY

CyberCash, located in Reston, Virginia, has been a key player in developing an online purchase-payment system. They've teamed up with certain banks and credit card companies to transfer money from your electronic "wallet" to the participating vendor's bank account. A transaction log also records all wallet activities.

There is no cost to the consumer for using the wallet, which can be downloaded from the CyberCash Web site (http://www.cybercash.com). You'll go through a simple registration process to confirm the validity and authenticity of your account. The rest is a simple click-through process.

You'll be comforted to know that the transaction is merely a legal record; the money stays safely within the confines of the existing banking networks and never really enters the "wallet."

Excite

Although it doesn't have the breadth of some of the other search engines, Excite (www.excite.com) has something the other sites don't have—reviews. This is a good way to find some of the better financial pages on the Web. You can also search by key word, including searches of Usenet (to find newsgroups). When you complete a search, you can tell the engine to find related Web documents and it will automatically do so.

Lycos and Point

Lycos (www.lycos.com) catalogs Web pages, but it is more selective than other search sites. It lists sites with heavy traffic or sites that pass through the scrutiny of its editorial staff. Search and find--related site functions can also be found at Lycos. It also offers Point (www.point.com), which includes reviews of the top 5 percent of sites on the Web.

Infoseek

Infoseek (www.infoseek.com) catalogs Web pages by category and also lets you do keyword searches. It's a little thin in the financial department.

Open Text

This Canadian-based search engine (index.opentext.net) does pretty much what the others do.

WebCrawler

WebCrawler (www.webcrawler.com) is another site that tries to select the "best" of the Web. The

Major Online and Internet Service Providers

There are many Internet Service Providers (ISPs). These are some of the major national companies. Check with local businesses and your local phone company as well. Prices of these services are subject to change. You should call the service to get the latest rates.

Service	Phone Number	Price/Mo.
America Online	(800) 827-6364	$19.95, plus other options
Microsoft Network	(800) 386-5550	$6.95 (5 hrs.) plus $2.50/hr.
Prodigy	(800) 776-3449	$19.95, plus other options
Prodigy Internet	(800) 213-0992	$19.95, plus other options
AT&T (AT&T long-distance customers only)	(800) 967-5363	$19.95 (5 hrs.)
Netcom	(800) 501-8649	$19.95
MCI (MCI One customers only)	(800) 950-5555	$19.95
Sprynet	(206) 957-8997	$19.95
GNN	(800) 819-6112	$14.95 (20 hrs.)
PSI	(800) 827-7482	$9 (9 hrs.)
UUNet	(800) 488-6384	$30 (25 hrs.)

site is run by GNN, which is owned by AOL. Its catalog is well organized. If you go to the Personal Finance section, you'll find nearly 20 different subtopics, including Mutual Fund choices.

Magellan

Magellan (www.mckinley.com) is a good site for browsing because it reviews and rates Web sites. Just click on the hotlink (usually underlined and blue) to get a full review of the site.

Online Sites of the Big Three

Some of the best places to get information about mutual funds is at the Web sites of the investment companies themselves. If one thing can be said about the mutual fund industry, it's that it is quick to adapt to whatever is state-of-the-art. Every day, more and more investment companies put up a Web site, and companies that already have sites continually experiment with ways to improve them.

And some of the best information can be found at the sites of the biggest companies such as Fidelity Investments, Charles Schwab, and Vanguard.

Fidelity Investments

With more than 3,000 pages of information at its Web site, Fidelity has set up a massive resource for mutual fund investors (www.fid-inv.com). It's estimated that Fidelity spends $2 million a year to maintain the site, which registers about 100,000 hits a day. At the beginning of 1997, Fidelity began a pilot project to allow its customers to trade online. You can get prospectuses for most of Fidelity's funds here, as well as all the other pertinent data on the company.

Charles Schwab & Co.

Although Schwab is a discount broker, it has become a force in the mutual fund industry by offering investors more than 1,100 funds from 150 well-known families. Their site is also mammoth, with 1,500 pages of information (www.schwab.com).

In addition to letting you download fund prospectuses, NAVs, and performance data, the site has interactive features such as a demonstration on buying and selling stocks online, and help on developing an investment plan. Schwab also has an all-electronic trading subsidiary—e.Schwab—which lets you trade funds at the flat rate of $29.95.

Vanguard Group

For the novice investor, Vanguard's site is a wish come true (www.vanguard.com). It boasts more than 1,000 pages and has excellent educational material. It even contains a "university" that offers courses to novice investors. Course modules include "What Is a Mutual Fund?" "Building a Portfolio," "Selecting Specific Mutual Funds," and "Mutual Funds and Taxation." If you open an account with Vanguard, you can check your account information online. And it is easier to navigate this site than those of other investment companies, because Vanguard has a created a nice site map.

Other Investment Company Sites

Almost every fund company has a Web site. We're not going to list them all, but here are some highlights of other sites that concentrate on individual funds.

Galt's NETworth

As more and more investment companies establish Web sites, NETworth has lost some of its standing (networth.galt.com). Nevertheless, you should check it out because more than 70 fund families have a presence there. These include Twentieth Century–The Benham Group, Calvert, Dreyfus, Janus, Safeco, and Scudder, Stevens & Clark. You can find prospectuses and fund profiles there, and set up a personal portfolio.

The American Association of Individual Investors is one of several organizations that provide the site with content. In addition to offering enlightening educational materials on mutual funds and investing, the association has a guide to finding investment software and a primer on how to use your computer for investing.

T. Rowe Price

It's one of the largest no-load fund families, and the site (www.troweprice.com) offers typical fund fare—NAVs, performance numbers, fund profiles, and prospectuses. One feature of note is the investment strategies documents in the site's library. Price has an online trading system, but it's only available to America Online subscribers.

Strong Funds

Even if you don't have an account with Strong, there are a couple of features at this site that will be of interest (www.strong-funds.com). Strong offers interviews with fund managers by using a technology called Real Audio. And it has some good asset allocation models that may give you some ideas about how to structure your portfolio.

Calvert

If you're interested in socially responsible investing, you should check out this site (www.calvertgroup.com). Calvert is a leader in managing funds that embrace this approach. It was also one of the first funds to allow its customers to have online access to their accounts.

GIT Funds

Getting a list of stocks that your fund holds on a daily basis is nigh impossible—unless you have an account with GIT. Each day, it uses its Web site (www.gitfunds.com) to post the current group of securities that are in the portfolios of each of its funds.

Discount Brokers Online

Even before the mutual fund companies began populating the Internet with Web pages, the discount brokerage houses charged into cyberspace with enthusiasm. With the exception of Schwab, the discounters sell other company's funds and charge you for it. Here are some of the major discount brokers on the Net.

Jack White & Co.

Some 4,200 funds can be purchased through mega-discounter Jack White (www.pawws.com/jwc). But the company isn't interested in small-time investors at its Web site. You'll have to invest at least $5,000 to open an account. White, like other discount brokers, charges flat fees for its services—$27 for a $5,000 transaction; $35 for a transaction between $5,001 and $25,000; and $50 for a transaction over $25,001.

National Discount Brokers

NDB (www.pawws.com/ndb) also requires a $5,000 minimum in accounts that trade online. It has a slightly higher fee schedule than Jack White, too. Fees range from $34 to $85. You can buy any fund through NDB, but it also offers more than 300 no-fee, no-load funds. A list of these funds is posted at the Web site. NDB's Web site includes a good FAQ (Frequently Asked Questions) page that explains its services.

Net Investor

Net Investor, a child of the Chicago Brokerage, Howe Barnes, has created a friendly Web site that's easy to navigate (www.pawws.com/tni). You'll need $5,000 to open an account here, too ($2,000 for an IRA), and fees range from $35 to $60. NI offers 2,900 funds, 700 of them no-loads. Funds can be traded at the Web site. Online services available to you when you open an account with NI include: information from such respected sources as S & P, First Call, and Lipper Analytical; historical price graphs of over 4,600 stocks and stock quotes; and reports on your account. (The reports also can be e-mailed to you automatically.) You can track the tax-lot cost basis of your portfolio, get a gain and loss report, and review details of all your transactions, including checking, dividends, and interest.

Lombard Securities

There is little mutual fund information at this site (www.lombard.com), but members of the general public can get delayed stock quotes and price and volume graphs of individual stocks for free. Lombard, which is a subsidiary of Thomas F. White in San Francisco, will set up an IRA for you for free and has a very low minimum of $500 to set up an account. *Barron's,* in its first ranking of discount brokers, rated Lombard number one.

OLDE Discount Brokers

There's no trading at this site (www.oldenet.com), but OLDE does offer funds from about 20 fund families. There's also some very terse educational material about investment strategies and why people invest in mutual funds. OLDE manages its own family of top-performing money market funds.

Quick & Reilly

Q & R has been offering online trading through America Online for some time (www.quick-reilly.com). Recently it brought its act to the Web. Although Q & R offers more than 1,500 fund options through its off-line facilities, it is only allowing stock trades via the Web at the moment. It says, however, it will have fund trading on the Internet soon. Even if you don't have an account with the discount broker, you can use its Portfolio Tracker feature to create up to ten portfolios for yourself, each containing up to 30 stocks. Also available to visitors to the site is a feature called Market Snapshot, which gives you the latest market news, indexes, statistics, graphs, and economic report needs. There is no minimum amount required to open an account. However, Q & R may require full payment or an acceptable deposit prior to the acceptance of any order. The minimum initial deposit to establish an interest-bearing money market account is $500.

PC Financial Network

PCFN pioneered online trading on the Prodigy Online service (www.pcfn.com). Now it has a Web presence, too. When you open an account with PCFN, you receive real-time quotes, news, access to your investment portfolio, and online trading of stocks, options, and over 5,000 mutual funds. In PCFN's FundCenter you can find detailed information and performance profiles from Lipper Analytical Services about the brokerage's mutual funds. You can also buy, sell, and exchange the funds online.

PCFN's FundScan, an interactive mutual fund screening and selection tool, lets you set your own criteria to choose from more than 5,000 mutual funds. PCFN doesn't charge any transaction fees for load funds and charges $35 for no-load and low-load funds. It charges $20 for exchanges between funds. To start an account through PCFN's Web site, you need a minimum of $5,000 ($1,000 for retirement accounts).

Accutrade

You can trade more than 5,000 funds at this site (www.accutrade.com). Pricing is reasonable. It costs nothing to buy funds with no-transaction fees. If you stay invested in the funds more than six months, there's no charge for redeeming or swapping your shares; if you hold your shares for fewer than six months, there's a $27 fee for redeeming or swapping your shares. Stock quotes are available to the general public at this site as well as a demo on how to trade online with Accutrade.

K. Aufhauser's WealthWeb

Aufhauser was one of the first discount brokerages to bring its service to the Web (www.aufhauser.com). It offered stock trading at the end of 1994 and opened up fund trading in 1995. Aufhauser clients also have the ability to purchase over 6,000 mutual funds, both load and no-load, over the Internet. For its account holders, Aufhauser has set up a Cyber University on the Web site, which is designed to demonstrate a few of the capabilities of online trading with the company. For transactions that involve no-load mutual funds, Aufhauser charges $34 for principal amounts up to $4,999; $40 for amounts from $5,000 to $9,999; and $50 for amounts of $10,000 or more.

Ceres Securities

Ceres has one of the lowest transaction rates—$18—on the Web for stock trades (www.ceres.com). Even if you don't have an account with Ceres, you can benefit from its Web site. Investment guru Andrew Tobias's daily column appears at the site. There's also an excellent tutorial on Internet basics here. You can enter a drawing and win a copy of Tobias's book, *The Only Investment Guide You'll Ever Need*. And you can try your hand at online trading with a demo. Ceres recently brought its trading show to America Online.

The Best of Other Online Resources

In addition to investment company sites and brokerage houses, there are plenty of independent sites that offer information and services to investors. It's a good idea to check them out because they don't have a vested interest in any particular family of funds. But be selective about what you read (remember, anyone can set up a site online). Here are some sites that are worth looking at.

The Finance Center

Of all the Web sites, this one is the snazziest (www.tfc.com). It uses multimedia—sound and music—to spruce up its presentation. It includes MarketMaven, a section (updated every Tuesday) that allows readers to discover what the top nationally recognized money managers and investment analysts have to say about the financial markets and individual stocks. There's also an online report on IPOs (initial public offerings), news on hot tech stocks, delayed stock information on industry groups, and a summary of financial news and rumors floating in cyberspace. The mutual fund section contains rankings of funds by objective and links to other fund sites. Definitely worth a bookmark in your Web browser.

INVESTools

This site (www.investools.com), operated by Tabula Interactive of San Francisco, is an easy way to find tools that will help you invest wisely. You can get free financial headlines from Reuters at the site (the full text of articles costs $.25 each, via CyberCash, an electronic cash payment system). Or you can buy all the articles on a particular company for $1. You can also get free stock price charts and stock quotes.

Information-packed Morningstar reports on individual funds are available here for $5 a pop. A number of financial newsletters are offered, but you'll have to pay for most of them. However, INVESTools posts its own free newsletter, which digests the best articles from its newsletter stable. Another free feature is Investors' Web Watch written by John Brobst of INVESTools. It gives both active and aspiring investors a view of the Web that is filtered to their needs. And there's a mutual fund discussion group at the site.

Mutual Funds Interactive

This site is dedicated entirely to mutual funds (http://www.brill.com/). It strives to publish original material that you won't find elsewhere. Features at the site include interviews with money managers, a moderated forum dedicated to mutual fund investors, and a section for new fund investors called Funds 101.

Interactive Nest Egg

Some of the information at this site (nestegg.idds.com) is dated and there are some links that no longer work. But some pearls remain. Its Fast Track feature gives you investment tips, such as how to select bonds for your personal portfolio. And the site provides a link to Zack's Investment Research, where you can find the daily earnings surprise—the companies that did better or worse than Wall Street analysts predicted; a portfolio alert, which will send the closing prices of up to ten stock or mutual funds via e-mail every day; and company reports that will give you a consensus of what analysts are saying about a company. The mutual fund center at the site contains a directory of more than 8,000 funds.

InvestorGuide

If you're looking for a good set of links to financial information on the Web, this is a good place to start (www.investorguide.com). Looking for a stock ticker for your Web browser? You'll find all the places you can download one here. Where can you get stock quotes? The sites for those services are listed here, too—as well as lots of other kinds of links.

Quicken Financial Network

This is a massive site (www.qfn.com) of financial information sponsored by Intuit, the makers of Quicken, the leading software package for managing personal finances. You can create a custom front page so when you log onto this site the latest prices of the stocks in your portfolio are displayed as well as news tailored to your interests. The site is linked to NETworth for its mutual fund information.

IBC Financial Data

This is the place to go for money markets (www.ibcdata.com) because IBC specializes in them. You can find rankings for the 20 highest-yielding retail money funds (taxable and tax-free), the 20 highest-yielding institutional money funds (taxable and tax-free), and the 15 largest retail money funds (taxable). You can also find special reports on the basics of investing in money market funds and bonds.

DBC

Data Broadcast Corp. has created a massive site of financial data here. You can get delayed quotes, stock charts, corporate reports filed with the SEC, and news. But the site isn't all business. It also has sports news and headlines and a link to the Wine Spectator, an online news source for oenophiles.

The Syndicate

The Syndicate (www.moneypages.com/syndicate) is the home of the mutual funds Usenet newsgroup (misc.invest.mutual-funds). When you join a newsgroup, you essentially become part of an e-mailing list for exchanges between people of like interests. It is a great way to share information you have, to ask questions, and to keep your ear to the ground. But remember to evaluate the information you receive before making big decisions. The site also contains links to other mutual fund sites, news about funds, and phone numbers for funds.

Telescan's Wall Street City

Another omnibus financial information site, Telescan's Wall Street City (http://www.wallstreetcity.com), includes a battery of search engines to scrutinize stocks in a myriad of ways—earnings, moving average, and so forth. Many of the services require subscription fees.

Fundscape

Calculating the return on a mutual fund portfolio can be complicated. That's why

Fundscape (www.fundscape.com) has created software to do it for you. The software is free and can be downloaded from this site. For a limited number of funds, the software will take the latest numbers relevant to your fund off the Internet and update your return for you automatically.

Mutual Fund Cafe

Mutual Fund Cafe (http://www.mfcafe.com/) concentrates on developments that affect the mutual fund industry. There's some material here for individual investors, but the location is geared to people with an interest in the business of mutual funds rather than the business of investing.

OF course, there are *always* TAXES

CHAPTER SEVENTEEN

Now you know the facts about mutual funds and how you can use them to help your **money multiply.** *But as everyone knows, when there's money to be made, it won't be long before the tax cats take their* **cut.**

Mutual fund companies actually pay almost no tax at all on the money they earn. That's because they pass the earnings on to you in the form of distributions—dividends and capital gains—and let you pay the taxes. Even if you choose to reinvest the distributions, you still have to claim it as income April 15.

Unless you have a tax-free mutual fund. Dividends from tax-free municipal bonds, for example, aren't subject to federal tax (although some states can tax them). Capital gains (the money you earn when you cash in a stock) are always taxed on all returns, even if it's a tax-free fund.

It's Inevitable

In January of each year, your mutual fund company will send you a form—Form 1099-B, Capital Gains (Losses)—telling you the total amount of capital gains or dividends that you received the year before. You must include that amount on your tax returns. You report the amount due Uncle Sam on Schedule D of your income tax return. Should you have any inappropriate ideas about reporting your capital gains, the 1099-B contains a helpful reminder that a copy of the form has been forwarded to the Internal Revenue Service. When you're finished with your 1099-B, file it in a safe place with the rest of your tax documents. You never know when you might need it in the future.

There are several ways to calculate a gain or loss in capital. The easiest way—and least likely to be questioned by the IRS—is to use the average cost method. The formula for figuring out the average cost of your shares looks like this:

AC = (CP + DR)/TS

You calculate the average cost of your shares (AC) by taking the cost of your shares (CP, the amount you've invested in the fund) and adding it to the dividends earned to that date (DR). Then you divide that sum by the total number of shares you held in that fund when you decided to sell.

Let's say you invest $5,000 early in the year. In May, you see that you have 200 shares of the fund and decide to redeem 100 of them. In that period, the fund returned $300 in dividends and the sale of your 100 shares amounted to $2,700. Plug those numbers into our formula so it looks like this:

($5,000 + $300)/200 = $26.50

Your average cost per share is $26.50. Your capital gain is the amount you received for the shares on the day you sold them (100 shares x $26.50 = $2,650) minus the average cost of those shares: $2,700 – $2,650 = $50. So you would pay taxes on $50. That $50 is what you report as a capital gain on schedule D of your tax return. If you experienced a loss, the result would be a negative one, but the method for arriving at that result would be the same.

Sometimes Timing Is Everything

Usually the answer to the question, "When should I buy a mutual fund?" is sooner rather than later, but tax-wary investors know that isn't the case. When you buy a fund, you don't want to buy it close to its ex-dividend date. That date, usually at the end of the calendar year, signals when a distribution is about to take place. If you buy shares just prior to that date, you'll have to pay taxes on the earnings even though you held your shares less than a year. If you buy your shares after that date, the net asset value of a fund's shares will have taken a "hit" from the distribution and will be selling at a lower price. This not only lets you buy more shares, but you can dodge the tax on the distribution, too.

For example, just prior to a distribution, you purchase $1,000 worth of shares in a fund. The fund has a net asset value of $25 per share, so you've got 40 shares. A $2 distribution is made. The NAV drops to $23. Your shares are worth $920. But you technically haven't lost any money because the distribution was worth $80 ($2 x 40 shares). However, you will lose money because that $80 is a capital gain, and you're going to have to pay tax on it at the end of the taxable year. If you bought your shares after the ex-dividend date, you'd end up with the same number of shares (assuming you invested what would have been the distribution into the fund), but you wouldn't have to worry about them producing a tax burden for you until the next distribution period rolled around, or probably in the next taxable year.

You can find out when a fund's ex-dividend date is and what the size of its distribution will be by calling the fund. If the distribution will be a small one, the advantage of buying the fund now may outweigh the tax consequences.

More Paperwork

Despite the government's paperwork reduction program, you'll receive a second form from your fund to go along with your capital gains material—form 1099-DIV, a report on your dividends. Even if the dividends aren't taxable, you still have to report them on your tax return. But don't worry. If they're not taxable, they won't be included as part of your income and you won't pay any taxes on them.

Every time your fund makes a distribution, it will send you written confirmation that such a distribution has been made. Keep these confirmations until you receive your year-end report from the fund. Then you can ditch them after verifying that the total amount is correct. Make sure, however, that you always retain the year-end report in your tax-return archives.

A Somewhat Free Lunch

If all this tax business rattles you, you can invest in tax-free mutual funds. Most investment companies offer them.

The portfolios of these funds are made up of municipal bonds, also known as munis. The volatility of munis varies along the lines of all bonds. The longer the term on the bond, the greater the risk. Munis with terms of four years or less are considered short-term and are the safest; munis with maturities from five to ten years are intermediate-term bonds, which are more volatile but have higher yields. The riskiest munis, but the ones with the greatest yields, run for more than ten years and their prices are the most volatile. Which kind of muni fund you should invest in depends on your risk tolerance. In addition to the plain vanilla muni-bond fund, there are insured tax-free funds. The insurance on these funds will protect you if the issuer of the bonds goes belly up; it won't protect you against fluctuations in the fund's NAV.

One obvious advantage to investing in a tax-free fund is that you don't have to pay any federal taxes on the dividends from the bonds in the fund.

A second advantage stems from the first: Because you don't pay any federal tax on the dividends, your yields can compete with those of taxable funds. A tax-free fund with a yield of 6 percent is the equivalent of an 8.3 percent yield from a taxable fund—if you're in the 28 percent tax bracket. Or it is the same as an 8.7 percent yield if you're in the 31 percent tax bracket. And that 6 percent could be considered a low yield. Riskier tax-free funds can return 10 percent, the equivalent of 13.9 percent from a taxable fund for the average taxpayer.

Calculating the benefits of investing in a tax-free fund is relatively simple. The formula looks like this:

$$TY = Y/(1 - TB)$$

In the formula, the yield you would need from a taxable fund (TY) to match the yield of a tax-free fund can be calculated by dividing the yield of the tax-free fund (Y) divided by one minus your tax bracket percentage (TB). If you're interested in a tax-free fund with a 9 percent yield and you're in the 28 percent tax bracket, when you plug those values into the formula, it would look like this:

$$TY = .09/(1 - .28)$$

So if you're in the 28 percent tax bracket, you would need to invest in a taxable fund that yields at least 12.5 percent.

You might ask yourself, "Why not cut out the middleman—the mutual fund—and invest directly in a muni myself?" For the small investor, this can be a problem since the minimum investment in a single muni issue is usually $5,000. And, remember the power of diversification. Even if you have the $5,000, you'd be investing it all in a single issue. With a mutual fund, your risk is spread over many issues. It's easy to find a mutual fund with insurance to cover the risk of a bond issuer that defaults on its bonds.

Thinking of Taxes When Picking a Fund

The reason you or anyone else invests in a mutual fund is to make money. So, after determining your risk tolerance, a fund's potential return-on-investment should carry the most weight in your decision to choose it. But when you're ready to make the final selection, it won't hurt to analyze how well your finalists manage their tax liability—because that will probably determine your own tax liability. For example, you wouldn't want a fund to make massive distributions into an account you had to pay taxes on, but you would want those kinds of distributions in an account you were using as an IRA.

Federal law effectively requires all mutual funds to distribute 98 percent of all the dividends and capital gains they realize every year. Just one more definition: The return a fund gives its investors before it makes its distributions is called its pretax return; its return after it makes its distributions is called after-tax return. This after-tax return divided by the fund's pretax return produces a "tax efficiency" ratio, which is shown on the prospectus. The more efficient a fund is in managing its tax liability, the less, theoretically, you should have to pay in taxes on capital gains and dividend distributions every year.

Tax efficiency, however, is a marginal issue, and if you are going to keep your fund for fewer than ten years, it won't be an issue at all for you. But you're no longer clueless about selecting funds. So the tax effect is something well worth considering.

SO *how* do you BEGIN?

CHAPTER EIGHTEEN

***You've got the skills. It's time to stop quivering and make some decisions. Look at the options, breathe in, breathe out, and take the* first step *toward assembling your investment* portfolio.**

All that really means is that you put together your own particular collection of investments. Let's put together what you've learned into three essential steps:

1. Set your goals (chapter three).
2. Decide what mix of funds (conservative, aggressive, and so on) will help you meet those goals (chapters five and fourteen) and how you want to allocate your money among them.
3. Sign up for specific funds (chapters twelve and thirteen).

Set Your Goals

The goal of all investing is to make money. But that's like saying the goal of all commercial airlines is to get from one point to another. If you boarded a plane in New York with the goal of reaching Los Angeles, and the plane reached L.A. seven days later, would you say you met your goal successfully? Probably not.

The same can be said for investing. To be successful, your goal must be more specific than just "making money." Whether you plan to finance your child's college education or to treat yourself to a 60-foot yacht, you probably can estimate the cost and anticipate a specific time to withdraw the money. It's true that a vague goal like "get rich quick and live a life of leisure," may inspire you to invest feverishly, but it's a goal that is a lot less likely to be satisfied.

So, when defining your goals, be realistic. You should cover your basic needs before you start diverting money into investments. And that includes arranging for insurance—life, auto, health, and casualty—before you gamble in the investment market.

Start by taking an inventory of your finances. Two traditional ways to do that is with a statement of net worth and a statement of income and expenses.

Your Net Worth

After you assess your own net worth, you'll have a pretty good picture of your present financial condition. With this picture you'll be able to mold realistic objectives for yourself. There are three key areas in the statement: liquid assets, productive assets, and your propensity to borrow.

Liquid assets are assets you can turn into cash immediately—think of them as your safety net, or money that isn't "frozen" and inaccessible. So you'll want this money to be in an account where the principal fluctuates slightly or not at all (such as a money market or a bank savings account). Of course, these are the accounts with the lowest return on your investment.

The rule of thumb is that liquid assets should equal three to six months of living expenses. But ultimately, it's up to you to find a number that makes you feel comfortable.

Productive assets have the potential to create income for you—and the extra income will help you achieve your investment goals. (But the fluctuating value means you can't guarantee access to your safety cushion should you need it.) The high-growth accounts, those that invest your assets in stocks and long-term bonds, can be an excellent way to increase your principal. So can long-term real estate investments—when market values go up.

Your productive assets should grow faster than your liabilities. The consequences are fairly obvious if they don't. That's why you want to pay off all credit card debt and high-interest consumer loans before diverting money into other investments. The interest rates on these nonproductive assets almost always exceed what you can expect your productive assets to return to you. It would be quite an achievement for any professional money manager to beat the typical 17 percent interest rate on some credit cards.

The final key component of the net worth statement is your propensity to borrow. That shows how likely you are to borrow to acquire assets. A propensity-to-borrow ratio of 35 percent, for example, indicates that you borrowed money to acquire 35 percent of your assets. The lower this number, the greater your net worth. Although it sounds odd that you would go into debt to increase your net worth, it might make sense if you use the money to acquire a productive asset (like a house).

The Income and Expense Statement

After you've completed your net worth statement, it is useful to create an income and expense statement. This is your meat-and-potatoes document.

Even if you are rolling in money, at some point you need to figure out what you have, what you spend, and exactly how much is left over for investing. When you sit down and analyze it that way, you can often identify expenses that you can eliminate, and divert the savings into your investment plan. Remember, the power of compounding means that even a small amount of cash can become a monster amount over a sufficient period of time. For example, an extra $100 a month invested over 20 years can become $100,000 in a portfolio that is designed to earn just under 11 percent a year. Without compounding, the same $100 per month would only add up to $24,000 if saved for the same period of time.

You Need to Plan Your Return on Investment

Time is an important element here. It determines the risk you'll have to assume to get the return you need to meet your goals. If your goal is one year away, you have to be more conservative than if your goal is five years away—even if your risk tolerance level is high. Why? Because you have very little margin for error. Once you decide on a goal and the time frame, you can calculate the return on investment you need to achieve it:

RR = ((\$W/\$H)^1/T) – 1

As usual, the required return formula looks more complicated than it is—even if it does have an exponent (^) in it. In the formula, you take the money you want (\$W) and divide it by the money you have (\$H). You take the result of that operation and raise to the power of 1 divided by the time you have (T) then subtract 1 from the result to arrive at your required return (RR).

So let's say you have \$25,000 and want to grow it to \$50,000 in seven years to buy a new house. If you pop those numbers into the formula, it would look like this:

RR = ((\$50,000/\$25,000)^1/7) – 1
= ((2)^.1428) – 1
= (1.104) – 1
= .104

You would need a 10.4 percent return to grow \$25,000 to \$50,000 in seven years.

Allocate Your Money

You've identified your goals. You know how much money you're going to invest. You know what kind of return you need to meet your goals. Now you have to decide what type of funds you need to invest in.

There are some basic tenets for choosing funds to meet your objectives. If you want maximum growth, you invest in small-company, or "small-cap," funds. If you're looking for growth with an element of stability, you invest in growth and income funds.

You might choose an international fund to diversify a portfolio—because, as we mentioned before, foreign stocks don't perform in tandem with U.S. stocks. And if you need to preserve a portion of your assets for a fixed income, you should be in money market or short-term bond funds. Of course, if you're in a high-tax bracket, you should look seriously at tax-free municipal bond funds.

If you asked a professional to help you allocate your assets, that adviser would probably start by asking your age and stage in life. Every investor is different, but it is likely that you can identify with one of the three groups described next.

Building Wealth

If you won't need the bulk of your investment assets soon, and you don't have a lot of responsibilities, then you can afford to invest in a portfolio that maximizes your return through long-term growth. You're not worried about preserving capital as much as you want to pump up your profits, so you'd arrange a portfolio using one of several fund mixes.

The growth and income approach aims to increase wealth while guarding against market surprises. The approach calls for you to invest 35 percent of your money in small-company funds for growth, 15 percent in international funds for growth and diversity and 60 percent in growth and income funds. Because the latter funds invest in seasoned companies that pay dividends, the dividends can be used to offset losses that are incurred by the riskier funds in the mix.

A more conservative approach is to bring money market and bond funds into the mix. Something like this: 13 percent in small-cap stocks, 27 percent in growth and income, 43 percent in international funds, and 17 percent in money market and short-term bond funds. With a portfolio like that, you have a 50-50 chance of earning 11 percent annually over the term of the investment.

Yet another approach for the aggressive investor would be to invest 50 percent of your money in aggressive funds and 25 percent in high-yield bonds. Then you would cushion yourself by investing the rest of your assets in money market funds.

Your Own Statement of Net Worth

ASSETS

Liquid

Checking account	______
Savings account	______
Money market	______
CDs	______
Stocks	______
Bonds	______
Mutual funds	______
Life Insurance (cash value)	______
Other	______

Nonliquid

IRAs	______
401(k)	______
Annuities	______
Other	______
Primary residence	______
Vacation property	______
Investment property	______
Car	______
Collectibles	______
Jewelry	______

Furniture	________
Clothing	________
Other	________
Total Assets	________
LIABILITIES	
Housing Loans	
Primary residence mortgage	________
Second mortgage	________
Vacation home mortgage	________
Investment property loan	________
Installment Loans	
Bank loans	________
Car loans	________
Student loans	________
Credit cards	________
Insurance premiums	________
Other loans	________
Total Liabilities	________
Net Worth (Total Assets – Total Liabilities)	________

Planning for a Family

Although a single person often can afford to invest aggressively, your plans might change when you join with someone else to form a family. You probably want your family's investment to grow, but want to reduce the risk of losing your principal. You may begin saving for retirement. And if you have children, you might want to plan for their educational needs.

However, families commonly make one of these mistakes: They chase the hot fund of the moment in pursuit of a killer return, or they overreact to the threat of risk by socking away their money in low-yielding investments. Either choice is extreme, when all you really need to do is moderate the risk.

A family's allocation strategy might still assign a significant proportion of assets to relatively risky, high-yielding funds. For instance, you could put 50 percent of your money in stocks that have proven, long-term track records. But make sure you've stashed about three months of expenses in money market funds. Whatever cash you have left can go into a short-term bond fund.

A slightly more aggressive approach would be to include some small-company stocks in your portfolio. This mix might be 9 percent in small company stocks, 19 percent in growth and income funds, 32 percent in international funds, and 40 percent in money market and short-term bonds.

If you would be more comfortable with a conservative approach, try this. It is a suggested allocation for a young couple with two incomes and one or two children. Thirty percent of the portfolio is invested in aggressive growth stock funds and 25 percent in moderately aggressive investments like high-yield bond and long-term growth funds. The remainder of the portfolio is shared between conservative investments—10 percent in tax-free money market funds and 35 percent in long-term municipal bond funds.

Approaching Retirement

As you close in on retirement, you'll want to preserve your capital. But you still need to keep building your assets because you're going to have to rely on it for 20 years or more. The combination of needs can make the investor who is approaching retirement

Your Own Statement of Income and Expenses

INCOME (after-tax)

Salary	________
Interest and dividend income	________
Other income	________

EXPENSES

Mortgage/rent and maintenance	________
Food, clothing, entertainment	________
Auto loan and maintenance	________
Utilities	________
Insurance (home, life, auto)	________
Medical	________
Installment loans	________
Credit card loans	________
Other loans	________
Other expenses	________

Net monthly income	________
Net monthly expenses	________
Net monthly surplus	________

feel a bit nervous. Often the reaction is pure panic, and years of wise investment techniques are shed in favor of market timing tactics.

Don't do it. A diversified strategy is still in order as retirement approaches. So your portfolio might look something like this: 35 percent of your money in a fund with growth stocks, 15 percent in international funds, 5 percent in inflation hedges, 10 percent in money markets, and 35 percent in bonds of differing maturities.

Or, invest the largest portion of the portfolio, 35 percent, in conservative vehicles such as longer-term municipal bonds. Another 30 percent is allocated to short-term, tax-free municipal bonds, 25 percent is in a moderately aggressive stock fund, and 10 percent is in a small-cap stock fund.

If you want to be a little more aggressive, you can mix in some small-cap funds. That kind of portfolio might be appropriated like this: 6 percent in small-company funds, 11 percent in growth and income funds, 21 percent in international funds, and 62 percent in money market or short-term bond funds.

Retired

When you retire, your allocation strategy should change again. You want your investments to produce income for you, and you want to preserve your principal. A common mistake is to let too much money sit in certificates of deposit (CDs) and bonds. That kind of strategy can hurt your purchasing power because you have to keep up with economic inflation and with health-care inflation, which is even higher. So you still need a growth component in your portfolio.

A portfolio that follows those guidelines might consist of 25 percent bonds, 25 percent money market funds, and 50 percent conservative growth vehicles (growth and income funds, utility stock funds, or high-dividend yielding funds).

A more conservative approach—but one that gives you a 50-50 chance of making an 8 percent return in a given year—calls for you to invest 18 percent of your money in growth and income funds, 12 percent in utility or income funds, and 70 percent in short-term or intermediate bond funds and money market funds.

Or allocate the largest portion of the portfolio to fixed income investments. For example, put 40 percent in money market funds, and another 35 percent in conservative stock funds to preserve capital and pad income. The remaining 25 percent could be invested in moderately aggressive growth funds to ensure that your purchasing power doesn't get eroded by inflation.

Sign Up for Your Funds

By using the knowledge you've gained from the earlier chapters in this book, and following some general guidelines, you should be able to pick the funds that meet your allocation guidelines. Here are some tips for picking funds.

- Don't buy more funds than you have to if you're a novice. Following funds can take time and you want to do the job properly. The fewer funds you have to follow, the better job you can do of following them.
- Select no-load funds when possible.
- Invest in funds that have track records. Look for funds that have been around for five years or more.
- Choose funds with expense ratios of 1 percent or less.
- Compare the fund to its peers. Has it outperformed them consistently for a year or more?
- Analyze the fund's manager. How long has the manager been in control of the fund? How has the fund performed under that manager? Are there any rumors that the manager is going to leave the fund?
- Buy funds with assets of at least $100 million. If there's a rash of redemptions, a well-endowed fund can handle the reduction better than one with a slimmer figure.

Once you invest in your funds, be vigilant. At a minimum, you should check your funds once a week. But don't be obsessive. Remember, you're in the game for the long term—at least five years—so it is a waste of energy to agonize daily over the NAVs.

Over the years, mutual funds have proven to be a solid investment vehicle for small and large investors alike. Even during recessionary periods mutual funds have managed to produce good returns for investors. If they can perform like that in bad times, imagine what they will do for you during good times. What are you waiting for? Get invested!

GLOSSARY

Accredited Personal Financial Planning Specialist (APFS): A financial planning designation indicating that a Certified Public Accountant (CPA) has passed a tough financial planning exam administered by the American Institute of Certified Public Accountants.

accumulation plan: A relatively easy method of buying mutual fund shares through small, regular, voluntary purchases.

ADY form: A form on file with the Securities and Exchange Commission that contains important financial information about a registered investment adviser.

aggressive growth fund: A mutual fund that seeks a high level of capital growth through investment techniques involving greater than ordinary risk. [See: capital appreciation funds.]

annual return: The yearly percentage of change in a mutual fund's net asset value.

appreciation: The growth of capital or principal investment.

asset allocation fund: A balanced fund in which changes are made in the stock and bond percentage mix, based on the outlook for each market.

automatic investment plan: A program that allows you to have as little as $50 a month electronically deducted from your checking account and invested in the mutual fund of your choice.

automatic reinvestment: An option available to mutual fund shareholders in which fund dividends and capital gains distributions are automatically reinvested back into the fund to purchase new shares (at the current NAV) thereby increasing the value of their account.

automatic withdrawal: An arrangement offered by many mutual funds that enables shareholders to receive fixed payments, generally monthly or quarterly. The actual payment is determined by the investor.

average maturity: The average time to maturity of securities held by a mutual fund. Changes in interest rates have greater impact on funds with a longer average life.

average price per share: The most popular method of paying taxes on mutual fund sales, in which gains or losses are calculated by first figuring an average cost per share. You calculate the total cost of all the fund shares you own and divide that by the number of shares you own.

back-end load: The fee paid when withdrawing money from a fund.

balanced fund: A mutual fund that diversifies its portfolio holdings by investing in common stocks, bonds, preferred stocks, and possibly other forms of investment. Holdings of defensive securities are proportionately increased when the market outlook appears unfavorable, and aggressive positions are stressed when the market seems to be headed upward.

bankers acceptance (BA): A short-term loan to companies that export worldwide. It is secured by goods that are to be sold.

basis point: The term used to describe the amount of change in yield. One hundred basis points equal 1 percent. An increase from 6 percent to 8 percent would be a change of 200 basis points.

bear market: When the market is moving lower on a fairly consistent basis for an extended period of time. During these periods, the stock market may lose more than 10 percent of its value.

beta: A measure of the relative volatility of a stock or mutual fund. The higher the beta, the more volatile the stock or fund is relative to the market as a whole. The Standard and Poor's 500 stock index is assigned a beta of one.

bid price: The price at which a mutual fund's shares are redeemed (bought back) by the fund. The redemption price is generally the current NAV per share excluding any load or commission.

blue-chip stock: The common stock of a major corporation that has a long, fairly stable record of earnings and dividend payments.

bond: A debt instrument issued by any company, city, state, or federal government and its agencies, with a promise to pay a predetermined rate of interest and to return the principal on a specified date.

bond fund: A mutual fund that has a portfolio consisting primarily of fixed income securities such as bonds. The fund's objective is normally steady income rather than capital appreciation.

bull market: When the market is moving higher on a fairly consistent basis for an extended period of time, generally two straight years or more.

callable debt: Debt that may be redeemed before it matures.

capital appreciation funds: Mutual funds that strive for maximum growth. Although these funds can earn the greatest gains, they also can rack up the heaviest losses. Also known as aggressive growth funds.

capital gains distributions: Payments made to mutual fund shareholders of profits realized by the fund on the sale of securities in the fund's portfolio. Such payments are usually distributed to the shareholders annually. These distributions are taxable to the shareholders (even in a tax-free fund).

capital growth: An increase in the value of a fund's portfolio as reflected in the NAV of the fund shares. Such growth is the objective of many mutual funds and their investors.

capital loss: A loss from the sale of a capital asset.

Certified Financial Planner (CFP): A financial adviser who obtains a license issued by the College of Financial Planning. This designation shows that the planner has had training in most financial areas including budgeting, taxes, savings, and insurance.

charitable lead trust: A legal account used to avoid estate taxes in which the named charity receives the investment income while the principal goes to the trust's beneficiaries.

charitable remainder trust: A legal account set up with a charity who pays the donor income for life. Upon death, the money goes to the charity, tax-free.

Chartered Financial Consultant (CHFC): Designation issued indicating completion of a program in financial, estate, and tax planning, in addition to investment management.

Chartered Life Underwriter (CLU): A designation issued indicating training in life insurance and personal insurance planning.

closed-end funds: Funds whose shares are traded on an exchange similar to that for stocks. The price per share doesn't typically equal the net asset value of a share.

commercial paper: Short-term loans to corporations.

commodities: Bulk goods, such as metals, oil, grains, and coffee, traded on a commodities exchange. Funds that invest in commodities futures are very volatile.

common stock: Unit of ownership in a public corporation with voting rights, but with lower priority than either preferred stock or bonds if the corporation goes bankrupt.

compound interest: Interest earned on the principal as well as on the previously accumulated interest.

diversification: The policy followed by mutual funds to reduce the risk inherent in investing by spreading investments among a number of different securities in a variety of industries.

dollar cost averaging: A strategy of making regular, set investments into a mutual fund and having the earnings automatically reinvested. This strategy reduces the average share costs to the investor who acquires more shares when the price is down and fewer shares when the price is up. Dollar cost averaging is voluntary on the part of the investor.

Dow Jones Industrial Average: The average of 30 blue-chip stocks, originally published in 1897. With some revisions it is still used today to show market trends.

Electronic Data Gathering, Analysis, and Retrieval (EDGAR): An electronic system implemented by the SEC that is used by companies to transmit all documents required to be filed with the SEC in relation to corporate offerings and ongoing disclosure obligations. EDGAR became fully operational mid-1995.

equities: Investments in stocks and other assets.

equity income funds: Mutual funds that favor investments in stocks that generate income over growth. As a result, they can be less risky than other types of stock funds.

Eurodollar CDs: CDs issued by U.S. banks that have branches in other countries. These tend to have higher yields than domestic CDs.

exchange privilege: The right to exchange shares of one mutual fund for shares of another fund under the same sponsorship at net asset value. This privilege is valuable when using market timing as a technique to improve your position relative to the market, or when your objectives change. This privilege may be exercised several times yearly, usually with no fee, or a very low fee.

ex-dividend date: The date on which the value of the income or capital gains distribution is deducted from the price of a fund's shares prior to the actual disbursement.

expense ratio: The percentage of a fund's assets that is paid out in expenses, including management fees, the cost of distributing literature, and the cost of administering the fund, divided by the average shares outstanding for the period. The average is around 1.5 percent.

face value: Value of a bond or note as given on the certificate. Corporate bonds are usually issued with $1,000 face values, municipal bonds with $5,000 face values, and government bonds with $1,000 to $10,000 face values. Also known as the principal.

Federal Deposit Insurance Corporation (FDIC): The federal agency that insures deposits up to $100,000 per account at member banks.

First-In-First-Out (FIFO): The basis for calculating the tax impact of mutual fund profits and losses that assumes shares sold are the oldest shares owned.

fixed income fund: Another term for a mutual bond fund.

401(k): An employee benefit plan into which employee contributions are made on a pretax basis. Both employer and employee contributions compound tax-free until withdrawn.

403(b): A tax-sheltered plan open to members of certain professions, for example, teachers and professors. It is similar to 401(k) plans; however, employers usually do not contribute to the 401(b) plan.

front-end loads: Sales commissions paid to purchase shares of mutual funds.

fund assets: The total market value of the assets invested by a fund.

general purpose money funds: Mutual funds that invest largely in bank CDs and short-term corporation IOUs called commercial paper.

global funds: Mutual funds that invest in both the United States and foreign countries. Also known as world funds or international funds.

GNMA funds: Mutual funds that have portfolios consisting of Government National Mortgage Association securities, known as Ginnie Maes.

government-only money funds: Mutual funds that invest in U.S. Treasury bills and short-term loans to the U.S. government. These are the least risky money funds because their investments are backed by Uncle Sam.

growth and income fund: A mutual fund that seeks both capital appreciation and current income. The portfolio of such a fund is balanced between stocks and fixed income securities.

growth funds: Mutual funds that invest in the stocks of well-established firms that are expected to be profitable and grow for years to come.

hedging strategy: A plan of investing in one or more securities to protect yourself from potential losses in other investments.

high-quality corporate bond funds: Mutual funds that buy bonds issued by the nation's financially strongest companies.

high-yield bond funds: Risky bond mutual funds that invest in high-yield bonds of companies with poor credit ratings. These bonds are rated below triple B by Standard & Poor's and Moody's. Also known as junk bond funds.

income fund: A mutual fund that has as its primary objective the production of income in the form of interest or dividends. Mutual funds that invest in preferred stock, bonds, Treasuries, and money markets are characterized as income mutual funds.

index funds: Mutual funds the portfolio of which duplicate the structure of either the Dow Jones Industrial Average or the Standard and Poor's 500 Composite Stock Price Index. Since it is difficult to beat the averages consistently, such a portfolio should at least match the performance of the indexes.

Individual Retirement Account (IRA): A retirement account established by individuals as a pension plan. Mutual funds have proved to be popular IRA investment vehicles. IRA accounts have several tax benefits as well.

inflation: A rise in the prices of goods and services.

installment investment strategy: An investment strategy in which you divide your investment among several mutual funds and make any new investments into the fund that performs the worst.

insured municipal bond funds: Mutual funds that invest in insured bonds issued by cities, towns, states, toll roads, schools, water projects, and hospitals. The interest income is tax-free, and the bonds are insured against default by large private insurance companies.

intermediate-term bond funds: Mutual funds that invest in bonds that mature in about five to ten years.

investment company: An organization that invests the pooled funds of its shareholders in securities appropriate to the fund's objectives.

junk bonds: High-yielding, noninvestment quality, lower-rated bonds of questionable worth.

junk bond funds: Mutual funds that invest in bonds issued by companies that are rated below BBB by Standard and Poor's or Moody's. Also known as high-yield bond funds.

Keogh accounts: Retirement accounts for self-employed individuals. They are similar to IRA accounts.

load: The commission paid by the investor when purchasing load mutual funds.

long-term bond funds: Mutual funds that invest in bonds that mature in more than ten years.

long-term gain: A gain on the sale of a capital asset where the holding period is six months or more and the profit is subject to the long-term capital gains tax.

market makers: The NASD member firms that use their own capital, research, retail, and/or systems resources to represent a stock and compete with each other when buying and selling the stocks. There are over 500 member firms that act as Nasdaq market makers. One of the major differences between the Nasdaq Stock Market and other major markets in the United States is Nasdaq's structure of competing market makers. Each market maker competes for customer order flow by displaying buy and sell quotations for a guaranteed number of shares. Once an order is received, the market maker will immediately purchase for or sell from its own inventory, or seek the other side of the trade until it is executed, often in a matter of seconds.

market surveillance: The department responsible for investigating and preventing abusive, manipulative, or illegal trading practices on the Nasdaq Stock Market.

market timing: A strategy by which investors attempt to buy low and sell high by buying when the market is turning bearish and selling at the end of a bull market.

money market fund: An open-ended mutual fund that invests in commercial paper, banker's acceptances, repurchase agreements, securities, certificates of deposit, and other highly liquid and safe securities, and pays interest at money market rates. The fund's net asset value remains a constant $1 a share, only the interest rate goes up or down. These tend to be lower-yielding, but less risky than most other types of funds.

municipal bond funds: Mutual funds that invest in tax-exempt bonds issued by states and local governments.

municipal bonds: Notes or other loans issued by state, city, or other local governments to pay for civic or other projects. All are exempt from federal taxes.

mutual fund: A fund operated by an investment company that raises money from shareholders and invests it in stocks, bonds, options, commodities, or money market securities.

National Association of Securities Dealers (NASD): The self-regulatory organization of the securities industry responsible for the regulation of the Nasdaq Stock Market and the over-the-counter markets.

net asset value (NAV): The market value of a fund share, synonymous with a bid price.

no-load fund: A mutual fund offered by an open-end investment company that imposes no sales charge (load) on its shareholders.

no-transaction fee account: A brokerage firm account that allows customers to purchase a selection of mutual funds with no charge or a limited charge.

open-end investment company: An investment company that continuously sells and redeems shares, i.e., a mutual fund.

over-the-counter market: The market that uses a network of brokers to buy and sell securities rather than an exchange.

portfolio: The total securities held by a mutual fund or a private individual.

portfolio manager: The person responsible for making mutual fund investments.

preferred stock: A type of stock that takes priority over common stock in the payment of dividends or disbursements if the company is liquidated.

preferred stock fund: A fund that has a portfolio consisting of shares of preferred stocks.

principal: Total amount of your initial investment plus subsequent investments (the total value of one's account excluding interest and dividends).

prospectus: A legal disclosure document that spells out information you need to know to make an investment decision about a mutual fund or other security.

rebalancing: An investment strategy in which you adjust your mix of investments periodically to keep the proper percentages of money in each fund based on your tolerance for risk.

record date: The date by which mutual fund holders (or other security holders) must be registered as share owners to receive a forthcoming distribution, e.g., dividends or capital gains.

redemption price: The amount per share mutual fund holders receive when they sell their shares (sometimes called the "bid price").

registered representative: A person licensed to sell stocks, bonds, mutual funds, and other types of securities.

return on investment (ROI): The percentage gain, including reinvestment of capital gains and dividends, if any.

S & P 500 Index: The measure of the performance of a selected large group of blue-chip stocks in the United States.

secondary market: The market where bonds, stocks, or other securities are bought and sold after they've been issued.

sector fund: A mutual fund that invests in only one segment of the market, such as energy, transportation, precious metals, health sciences, or international stocks. Also called specialty funds.

securities: Stocks, bonds, or rights to ownership, such as options, typically sold by a broker.

Securities and Exchange Commission (SEC): The federal agency created by the Securities Exchange Act of 1934 to administer that act and the Securities Act of 1933. The statutes administered by the SEC are designed to promote full public disclosure and protect the investing public against fraudulent and manipulative practices in the securities markets. Generally, most issues of securities offered in interstate commerce or through the mails must be registered with the SEC.

Securities Investor Protection Corporation (SIPC): A corporation backed by federal guarantees that provide protection for customers' cash and investments on deposit with an SIPC member firm, should the firm fail. Protection is generally provided up to $500,000.

share: A unit of ownership.

shareholder: One who owns shares. In a mutual fund, this person has voting rights.

short interest: The total number of shares of a security that have been sold short by customers and securities firms. [See: short selling.]

short selling: Short selling is the selling of a security that the seller does not own, or any sale that is completed by the delivery of a security borrowed by the seller.

short-term bond funds: Mutual funds that generally invest in bonds that mature in less than three years.

short-term gain: The gain realized from the sale of securities or other capital assets held six months or less.

short-term paper: Short-term loans to corporations or governments. Interest rates paid to mutual funds on such loans will vary with market conditions. Short-term paper is one of the primary sources of income for money market mutual funds.

Simplified Employee Pension Plan (SEP): A retirement plan that permits tax-deferred investments for self-employed individuals.

single-state municipal bond funds: Mutual funds that invest in the bonds of a single state so that investors avoid paying both state and federal taxes on their interest income.

small company stock funds: Volatile mutual funds that invest in younger companies with stocks that are frequently traded on the over-the-counter stock market.

socially responsible funds: Mutual funds that invest in companies that are politically and environmentally responsible. They will not own tobacco or alcohol stocks, nor invest in companies with poor employee relations.

speculation: Gambling on a risky investment in hopes of a high payoff down the road.

stock fund builder: An investment strategy in which you invest your bond fund's interest income into a stock fund to build your wealth.

stock symbol: A unique four- or five-letter symbol assigned to a stock security. If a fifth letter appears, it identifies the issue as other than a single issue of common stock or capital stock.

systematic withdrawal: A plan that permits you to withdraw a specified amount from your mutual fund account at regular intervals, generally on a monthly basis. This is a way of converting your investments into regular income.

tax avoidance: Any legal action that may be taken to reduce, defer, or eliminate tax liabilities.

taxable bond funds: A bond mutual fund in which interest income is taxed by the federal government.

tax-deferred investment: An investment that is not taxed until money is withdrawn, usually at retirement.

tax shelter: An investment used for deferring, eliminating, or reducing income taxes.

tenancy-by-the-entirety: A joint form of ownership that exists when the names of both husband and wife appear on the title of the property, each having rights of survivorship.

tenancy-in-common: Property or other capital assets jointly held by two people, usually unmarried, wherein each person retains control over his or her share of the property.

total return: The rate of return on an investment, including reinvestment of distributions.

transfer agent: An entity that maintains shareholder records, including purchases, sales, and account balances.

Treasury bills: Short-term Treasury IOUs.

trust: A legal document that does not have to be approved by probate court before your survivors can inherit your wealth.

trading halt: The temporary suspension of trading in a security, usually for 30 minutes while material news from the issuer is being disseminated over the news wires. A trading halt gives all investors equal opportunity to evaluate news and make buy, sell, or hold decisions on that basis.

12b-1 fee: A fee assessed shareholders by the mutual fund for some of its promotional expenses. A 12b-1 fee must be specifically registered as such with the Securities and Exchange Commission (SEC) and the fact that such charges are levied must be disclosed. (Not all mutual funds charge such fees.)

value averaging investing: An investment strategy in which you always make sure that the value of your fund increases by a specific amount over a specific time period.

variable annuities: An insurance program that allows you to direct your investment in a choice of mutual funds. Meanwhile, you get tax deferment of your earnings and a death benefit guarantee, and you are able to obtain periodic checks for life.

volatility: The tendency of a fund to rise or fall sharply in value.

wash sale: A strategy in which a security is bought back within 31 days after it is sold, "washing out" any capability of writing off losses on income taxes.

wire transfer: The use of a bank to send money to a fund or vice versa through a type of electronic transfer.

yankee dollar CDs: Debt instruments issued by some of the largest foreign banks in the world that have offices in the United States. They often yield slightly more than U.S. bank CDs.

zero-coupon Treasury bond funds: Mutual funds that invest in a certain type of Treasury security that provides no monthly income but instead pays the investor both accumulated income and principal at the bond's maturity.

RESOURCES

Books

The Beardstown Ladies Common-Sense Investment Guide. The Beardstown Ladies Investment Club with Leslie Whitaker (Hyperion, 1994).

Beating the Dow. Michael O'Higgins (HarperPerennial, 1992).

Beating the Street. Peter Lynch with John Rothchild (Fireside, 1994).

The Budget Kit. Judy Lawrence (Dearborn Financial Publishing, 1997).

Buying Mutual Funds for Free. Kirk Kazanjian (Dearborn Financial Publishing, 1997).

Everyone's Money Book. Jordan E. Goodman (Dearborn Financial Publishing, 1997).

How the Stock Market Works. John M. Dalton, ed. (The New York Institute of Finance, 1993).

How to Make Money in Stocks. William J. O'Neil (McGraw-Hill, 1995).

The Motley Fool Investment Guide. David and Tom Gardner (Simon & Schuster, 1996).

Mutual Fund Investing on the Internet. Peter Crane (Ap Professional, 1997).

NAIC's Investors Manual. 15th ed., Helen McLane (NAIC, 1992).

One Up on Wall Street. Peter Lynch, with John Rothchild (Penguin Books, 1989).

The 100 Best Mutual Funds to Own in America, Second Edition. Gene Walden (Dearborn Financial Publishing, 1997).

Terry Savage Talks Money: The Common Sense Guide to Money Matters. Terry Savage (HarperPerennial, 1991).

Magazines and Newspapers

Barron's. 200 Liberty St., New York, NY 10281, (800) 568-7625, $145/yr., weekly.

BusinessWeek. 1221 Avenue of the Americas, New York, NY 10020, (800) 635-1200, $49.95/yr., weekly.

Financial World. 1328 Broadway, New York, NY 10001, (800) 829-5916, $27/yr., 18 issues.

Forbes. 60 Fifth Avenue, New York, NY 10011, (800) 888-9896, $57/yr., biweekly.

Fortune. P.O. Box 60001, Tampa, FL 33660, (800) 621-8000, $57/yr., biweekly.

Inc. P.O. Box 54129, Boulder, CO 80332, (800) 234-0999, $19/yr., 18 issues.

Individual Investor. P.O. Box 680, Mt. Morris, IL 61054, (800) 383-5901, $22.95/yr., monthly.

Investor's Business Daily. 12655 Beatrice Street, Los Angeles, CA 90066, (800) 831-2525, $189/yr., daily.

Kiplinger's Personal Finance. 3401 East-West Highway, Hyattsville, MD 20782, (800) 544-0155, $19.95/yr., monthly.

Money. P.O. Box 60001, Tampa, FL 33660, (800) 633-9970, $39.95/yr., 13 issues.

The New York Times. P.O. Box 2047, S. Hackensack, NJ 07606, (800) 631-2500, $374.40/yr., daily.

Smart Money. P.O. Box 7538, Red Oak, IA 51591, (800) 444-4204, $24/yr., monthly.

The Wall Street Journal. 200 Liberty Street, New York, NY 10011, (800) 568-7625, $175/yr., daily (five days per week).

Worth. P.O. Box 55420, Boulder, CO 80322, (800) 777-1851, $18/yr., 10 issues/yr.

Mutual Fund Newsletters

Jay Schabacker's Mutual Fund Investing. 7811 Montrose Rd., Potomac, MD 20854.

Money Fund Expense Report, Money Fund Report. 290 Eliot St., P.O. Box 9104, Ashland, MA 01721, (508) 881-2800.

Mutual Fund Forecaster. The Institute for Econometric Research, 2200 SW 10th St., Deerfield Beach, FL 33442, (954) 421-1000.

Mutual Fund Letter. Investment Information Services, Inc., 680 North Lake Shore Dr., Suite 2038, Chicago, IL 60611, (312) 669-1650.

No Load Fund Analyst. 4 Orinda Way, Ste. 2300, Orinda, CA 94563, (510) 254-9017.

Stockmarket Cycles. P.O. Box 6873, Santa Rosa, CA 95406, (707) 579-8444.

Online Resources

American Stock Exchange Web site, http://www.amex.com

Bloomberg Web site, http://www.bloomberg.com

BulletProof Investor's Web site, http://www.bulletproof.com

BusinessWeek Web site, http://www.mcgraw-hill.com/business-economics/bwol.htm

Ceres Securities Web site, http://www.ceres.com

Chicago Board of Trade Web site, http://www.cbot.com

Chicago Mercantile Exchange Web site, http://www.cme.com

Chicago Stock Exchange Web site, http://www.chicagostockex.com

Crain's Chicago Business Web site, http://www.bizpubs.org/chicago.htm

Doug Gerlach's Invest-O-Rama Web site, http://www.investorama.com

EDGAR Web site, http://www.edgar.whowhere.com/

E*TRADE Web site, http://www.etrade.com

Federal Trade Commission Web site, http://www.ftc.gov

Fidelity Web site, http://www.fid-inv.com

Financenter Web site, http://www.financenter.com/

FTSE International Web site, http://www.ftse.com

Fundscape Web site, http://www.fundscape.com

Gabelli Funds Web site, http://www.gabelli.com

Goldman Sachs Web site, http://www.gs.com

Hoover's Online Web site, http://www.hoovers.com

Internal Revenue Service Web site, http://www.irs.ustreas.gov

Investment Brokerages Guide Web site, http://www.cs.cmu.edu/~jdg/invest_nrokers/index.html

Investor's Edge Web site, http://www.irnet.com

Investor Web site, http://www.investorweb.com

Lebenthal Web site, http://www.lebenthal.com

Legg Mason Web site, http://www.leggmason.com

Lombard Institutional Brokerage Web site, http://www.lombard.com

London Stock Exchange AIM (Alternative Investment Market) Web site, http://www.stockex.co.uk/aim

Merrill Lynch Web site, http://www.ml.com

Morgan Stanley Web site, http://www.ms.com

Motley Fool Web site, http://www.fool.com

Mutual Fund Cafe Web site, http://www.mfcafe.com/

Mutual Funds Magazine Web site, http://www.mfmag.com

Nasdaq Stock Market Web site, http://www.nasdaq.com

NETworth Web site, http://networth.galt.com

New York Mercantile Exchange Web site, http://www.nymex.com

New York Stock Exchange Web site, http://www.nyse.com

New York Times Web site, http://www.nytimes.com/

Paris Bourse Web site, http://www.bourse-de-paris.fr

PAWWS Financial Network Web site, http:/www./pawws.secapl.com

Philadelphia Stock Exchange Web site, http://www.phlx.com

Piper Jaffray Web site, http://www.piperjaffray.com

Prudential Securities Web site, http://www.prusec.com/

Quicken Financial Network Web site, http://www.qfn.com/index.html

Quicken Investment Center Web site, http://www.qfn.cominvest/

Quote.com Web site, http://www.quote.com

Salomon Brothers Web site, http://www.salomon.com

Schwab Web site, http://www.schwab.com

Securities and Exchange Commission Web site, http://www.sec.gov

Silicon Investor Web site, http://www.techstocks.com

Stein Roe Web site, http://www.steinroe.com

Stock Smart Web site, http://www.stocksmart.com

T. Rowe Price Web site, http://www.troweprice.com

Tokyo Stock Exchange Web site, http://www.tse.or.jp/

Vanguard Web site, http://www.vanguard.com

Wall Street Journal Web site, http://www.wsj.com

Worth Web site, http://www.worth.com

National Securities Regulators

Commodity Futures Trading Commission. (202) 418-5320 (enforcement division).

National Association of Securities Dealers. (202) 728-8000 (main), (800) 289-9999 (information about brokers and firms).

National Futures Association. Disciplinary Information Access Line (DIAL), 200 W. Madison St. Suite. 1600, Chicago, IL 50505, (800) 621-3570 (national), 800-572-9400 (in Illinois).

U.S. Securities and Exchange Commission. (202) 942-7040 (main), (800) SEC-0330 (investor information service).

Investment Clubs

National Association of Investors Corporation. 711 W. Thirteen-Mile Rd. Madison Heights, MI 48071. (810) 583-6242. For listings of local investment clubs in your area.

Associations and Organizations

American Association of Individual Investors. 625 N. Michigan Ave., Suite 1900, Chicago, IL 60611, (312) 280-0170, Web site: http://www.aaii.org/

American Stock Exchange. 86 Trinity Pl., New York, NY 10006, (212) 306-1000, Web site: http://www.amex.com

Dun & Bradstreet. 899 Eaton Ave., Bethlehem, PA 18025, (800) 234-3867, Web site: http://www.dbisna.com/dbis/purchase/tpurchas.htm

Investment Company Institute. 1401 H St., N.W., Suite 1200, Washington, DC 20005, (202) 326-5872.

National Association of Investors Corp. P.O. 220, Royal Oak, MI 48068, (810) 583-6242.

National Association of Securities Dealers. 1818 N St., N.W., Washington, DC 20036, (800) 289-9999, Web site: http://www.nasdr.com

National Center for Financial Education, P.O. Box 34070, San Diego, CA 92163, (619) 232-8811.

National Fraud Information Center. P.O. 65868, Washington, DC 20035, (800) 876-7060, Web site: http:/www.fraud.org

New York Stock Exchange. 11 Wall St., New York, NY 10005, (212) 656-3000. Web site: http://www.nyse.com

North American Securities Administrators Association. One Massachusetts Ave., N.W., Suite 310, Washington, DC 20001, (202) 737-0900.

Securities and Exchange Commission. Office of Investor Education & Assistance, 450 Fifth St., N.W., Washington, DC 20549, (202) 942-7040, Web site: http://www.sec.gov

INDEX